Blackstone Griddle Cookbook

Joe Wilcher

© **Copyright 2023 - All rights reserved**.

This document is geared towards providing exact and reliable information regarding the topic and issue covered.

- From a Declaration of Principles, accepted and approved equally by a Committee of the American Bar Association and a Committee of Publishers and Associations.

It is not legal to reproduce, duplicate, or transmit any part of this document in either electronic means or printed format. All rights reserved.

The information provided herein is stated to be truthful and consistent in that any liability, in terms of inattention or otherwise, by any usage or abuse of any policies, processes, or directions contained within is the solitary and utter responsibility of the recipient reader. Under no circumstances will any legal responsibility or blame be held against the publisher for any reparation, damages, or monetary loss due to the information herein, either directly or indirectly.

Respective authors own all copyrights not held by the publisher.

The information herein is offered for informational purposes solely and is universal as so. The presentation of the information is without a contract or any type of guarantee assurance.

The trademarks that are used are without any consent, and the publication of the trademark is without permission or backing by the trademark owner. All trademarks and brands within this book are for clarifying purposes only and are owned by the owners themselves, not affiliated with this document.

Contents

Introduction: 2

Advantages and Features of Cooking on a Gas Grill: 3

Tips and Tricks for Preparing and Using the Gas Grill: 5

Cleaning the Grill: 7

Recommended accessories and equipment 9

Breakfast and Brunch 11

   1. Cornmeal pancakes 12
   2. Denver Omelet Salad 12
   3. Apple Cinnamon Overnight Oats 13
   4. S'mores Waffle Sandwich 13
   5. Chia Pudding 14
   6. Grilled Chicken Pita 14
   7. Savory Hot Cereal with Apple 15
   8. Strawberry-Cherry Smoothie 15
   9. Simple Scrambled Eggs 16
   10. Roasted Mango with Vanilla Yogurt 16
   11. Ham & Brie Croissant Sandwich 17
   12. Summer Fruit Trifle 17
   13. Roasted Asparagus with Parmigiano-Reggiano 18
   14. Crunchy French Toast 18
   15. Sweet Potato and Egg Skillet 19
   16. Waffle Breakfast Sandwich 19
   17. Hash Brown & Egg Bake 20
   18. Potato Frittata 20
   19. Mango on Multigrain Toast 21
   20. Breakfast Burritos 21
   21. Egg & Cheese Bagel Sandwich 22
   22. Easy Egg Drop Soup 22
   24. Avocado Toast with Soft-Boiled Egg 23
   25. Peach Gazpacho 23

Appetizers and Side Dishes 24

   1. Guacamole 25
   2. Classic Deviled Eggs 25
   3. Fried Cabbage 26
   4. Savory Dates 26
   5. Tropical Fruit Salad 27
   6. Quinoa with Peas and Onion 27
   7. Sweet Corn Dish 28
   8. Crispy Baked Onion Rings 28
   9. Grilled Corn on the Cob 29
   10. Glazed Sweet Potatoes 29
   11. Hummus 30
   12. Apple Chips 30
   13. Smoked Salmon Pinwheels 31
   14. Grilled Peach Salsa 31
   15. Asian Cucumbers 32
   16. Grilled Cauliflower Wedges 32
   17. Chicken Dijon 33
   18. Brussels Sprouts with Pecans 33
   19. Macaroni salad 34
   20. Flavorful Green Rice 34

Salads and vegetarian dishes 35

   1. Carrot Salad 36
   2. Vegetable Korma Recipe 36

3. Pasta Vegetable Salad 37
4. Lemony Chickpeas 37
5. Rainbow Hash 38
6. Warm Cabbage, Fennel, and Pear Salad 38
7. Arugula & Brown Rice Salad 39
8. Ginger-Kale Smoothies 39
9. No-Cook Tomato Sauce 40
10. Mango Salad with Mint Yogurt Dressing 40
11. Tangy Curry Pasta Salad 41
12. Vegetable Salad Recipe 41
13. Buko Salad Recipe 42
14. Mango-Peach Smoothie 42
15. Mushroom & Zucchini Pesto Saute 43
16. Hearty Asian Lettuce Salad 43
17. Apple-White Cheddar Grilled Cheese 44
18. Zucchini Pancakes 44
19. Grilled Mixed Fruit & Vegetable Kabobs 45
20. Fruit Crisp 45

Fish and Seafood 46
1. Fish Dreams Recipe 47
2. Fish Stock Recipe 47
3. Sea Scallops Sauteed with Mushrooms & Pasta 48
4. Grilled Shrimp in the Shell 48
5. Grilled Scallop Kabob 49
6. Grilled Oysters 49
7. Soft Shell Crab Sandwich 50
8. Sea Scallops Brochette with Pernod Sauce 50
9. Fish Bake 51
10. Seafood Omelet 51
11. Szechuan Shrimp with Mushrooms & Peppers 52
12. Pan-Seared Salmon with Mustard Sauce 52
13. Horseradish Crusted Salmon 53
14. Salmon with Pesto 53
15. Sea Bass with Citrus-Olive-Caper Sauce 54

Burgers 55
1. Double cheeseburger 56
2. Mediterranean turkey burger 56
3. Zinger burger 57
4. Spicy Mexican bean burger 57
5. Bistro Burger 58
6. Cherry and Brie Burger 58
7. Veggie Tuna Burger 59
8. Chicken burger 60
9. Smash Burger 60
10. Chicken Caesar burger 61
11. Spinach Feta Burger 61
12. Chicken Cheese Burger 62
13. Tandoori chicken burger 62
14. Chicken Cordons Bleu burger 63
15. Turkey burger with special sauce 63
16. Vegan black bean burger 64
17. Steakhouse Burger 64
18. Burger with grilled onion 65
19. Homemade Beef Burger 65
20. Zesty Onion Burger 66
21. Chicken Chili Burger 66
22. Chicken Parmesan Burger 67
23. Zeus Burger 67

- 24. Greek Style chicken burger — 68
- 25. Cheddar Chicken burger — 68

Pork — 70

- 1. Pork Chops — 71
- 2. Pork loin crunch in red wine — 71
- 3. Pork Taquitos — 72
- 4. Pork tenderloin stir fry with Tangerines — 72
- 5. Pulled pork sandwich — 73
- 6. Pork sausage gravy — 73
- 7. Pork Sausage with lentils — 74
- 8. Pork Chops and apple bake — 74
- 9. Pork Stew — 75
- 10. Pork Chow Mein — 75
- 11. Skillet pork chops with carrot and pearl onion — 76
- 12. Garlic Lime Pork with spinach — 76
- 13. Pork Chops with Garlicky Broccoli — 77
- 14. Pork Pot Pie — 77
- 15. Pork Rice Stir-Fry — 78
- 16. BBQ Pork Chops — 78
- 17. Shredded Pork Tacos — 79
- 18. Chinese pork tenderloin — 79
- 19. BBQ Pulled Tuna Sandwich — 80
- 20. Pork sandwich spread — 80
- 21. Pork Sausage patties — 81
- 22. Pork Sausage and apple patties — 81
- 23. Pork Chops and bean Bake — 82
- 24. Pork Lo Mein — 82
- 25. Pork Jerky — 83
- 26. Pork Loin Stuffed with Spinach — 83
- 27. Pork chop with creamy mushroom sauce — 84
- 28. Pork and green bean stir-fry — 84
- 29. Pork Butt Roast with Vegetable — 85
- 30. Pork Fried Rice — 85

Poultry — 87

- 1. Brown rice, Leek, and stir-fried chicken — 88
- 2. Baked Parmesan Cheese Chicken — 88
- 3. Chicken Vegetable Stew — 89
- 4. Chicken curry — 89
- 5. Chicken Rice — 90
- 6. Lemon Herb Roast Chicken — 90
- 7. Chicken Bhuna Masala — 91
- 8. Chicken Protein Pots — 91
- 9. Air fried chicken general Tso's burger — 92
- 10. Chicken club wraps — 92
- 11. Chicken Stew in a Skillet — 93
- 12. Chicken Shashlik — 93
- 13. Fried Chicken — 94
- 14. Crispy Skinned Baked Chicken Drumstick — 94
- 15. Pon Pon Chicken — 95
- 16. Thai Chicken Curry — 95
- 17. Baked Salsa Chicken — 95
- 18. Roast chicken breast with Garbanzo beans — 96
- 19. Grilled Chicken with White BBQ Sauce — 97
- 20. Chicken quinoa bowl with olives and cucumber — 97
- 21. Chicken Quinoa Casserole — 98
- 22. Baked Chicken Tenders — 98
- 23. Chicken Quesadilla — 99
- 24. Chicken Jalfrezi — 99
- 25. Chicken Patties with mashed potato — 100

Beef 101
- 1. Black Bean and Beef Tostadas 102
- 2. Tomato Hamburger Soup 102
- 3. Burger Americana 103
- 4. Asian Beef and Noodles 103
- 5. Smothered Burritos 104
- 6. Beef and Broccoli 104
- 7. Slow Cooker Beef Stew 105
- 8. Beef and Vegetable Soup Recipe 105
- 9. Beef and Guinness Stew 106
- 10. Beef and Sweet Potato Curry 106
- 11. Beef and Spinach Lasagna 107
- 12. Beef and Cabbage Soup 107
- 13. Beef and Cheese Quesadillas 108
- 14. Ravioli Lasagna 108
- 15. Mexican Stuffed Peppers 109
- 16. Pizza Roll-Ups 109
- 17. Beefy Tortellini Skillet 110
- 18. Super Spaghetti Sauce 110
- 19. Beef Stir-Fry with Vegetable 111
- 20. Chili Con Carne 111
- 21. Beef and Mushroom Stroganoff Recipe 112
- 22. Beef and Rice Skillet Recipe 112
- 23. French Onion Beef Soup 113
- 24. Roasted Mango with Vanilla Yogurt ... 113
- 25. Classic Meatloaf 114

Pizza and Pasta Dishes 115
- 1. Spaghetti with Meatballs 116
- 2. Penne alla Vodka 116
- 3. Baked Ziti 116
- 4. Margherita Pizza 117
- 5. Hawaiian Pizza 117
- 6. Vegetarian Pizza 118
- 7. Lemon Butter Pasta with Asparagus .. 118
- 8. Carbonara Spaghetti 119
- 9. Fettuccine Alfredo 120
- 10. Garlic Shrimp Linguine 120
- 11. Creamy Chicken and Broccoli Alfredo 121
- 12. Pepperoni Pizza 121
- 13. BBQ Chicken Pizza 122
- 14. Four Cheese Pizza 122
- 15. Tomato and Basil Spaghetti Recipe: ... 123

Conclusion: 124

Introduction:

Thank you for visiting the Blackstone Griddle Cookbook! The versatility and convenience of cooking on a gas barbecue are celebrated in this cookbook. This cookbook has something for everyone, with over 200 recipes spanning everything from breakfast and brunch to pizza and pasta dishes. is a classic cooking method that has been used for generations. Grilling has changed throughout time from cooking over an open flame to using current gas grills. It is a wonderful way to prepare food because it enhances the natural flavors of the Materials and creates a distinct and delicious taste. Many household and professional cooks prefer gas grills because they provide exact temperature control, making it easy to cook food and preventing griddle cooking. The grill cookbook is intended to assist you in becoming a grill master, regardless of your level of experience. This cookbook will equip you with the knowledge and inspiration you need to produce tasty and nutritious meals on your gas barbecue, whether you're a seasoned grill master or a novice. Breakfast and brunch foods, appetizers and side dishes, salads and vegetarian meals, fish and shellfish, burgers, chicken, pig, beef, pizza, and pasta dishes are all covered. Each recipe in this cookbook is written with step-by-step directions and precise ingredient lists in mind. We've also included some handy hints and ideas to help you get the most out of your gas barbecue. We want to make sure you have all the knowledge you need to become a grill expert, from understanding the best cooking temperature for each type of food to using direct and indirect heat.

We feel that cooking on a gas grill is not only a convenient but also a healthier way to prepare food. Excess fat drips from the meal while grilling, lowering the overall fat level. Gas grills also allow you to cook with less oil, which might help you save calories in general. You may enjoy tasty and nutritious recipes that are good for you and your family with the Blackstone Griddle Cookbook. We've included recipes for a wide range of cuisines and flavors in this cookbook, from classic American burgers to Italian pasta meals. This cookbook contains something for everyone, whether you're cooking for a family dinner or throwing a backyard BBQ.

We hope you'll use the Blackstone Griddle Cookbook as your go-to guide for cooking on your gas barbecue. With over 200 tasty and simple-to-follow recipes, this book is likely to become a kitchen standard.

Let's light the grill and get to work!

Advantages and Features of Cooking on a Gas Grill:

Gas grill cooking is getting increasingly popular, and for good reason. Grilling on a gas grill offers various benefits and characteristics that make it a popular form of cooking for many people. In this section, we'll look at the benefits and features of cooking on a gas grill, as well as why it might be the ideal option for your next outdoor cooking trip.

1. Ease of use

One of the most significant benefits of cooking on a gas barbecue is its convenience. Gas grills are simple to start and heat up quickly, making them ideal for last-minute outdoor barbecues or dinner parties. They eliminate the need to start a fire or wait for charcoal to heat up, giving you more time to enjoy your cuisine and company. Furthermore, many gas barbecues include features such as side burners, built-in thermometers, and storage compartments to make grilling even easier.

2. Accurate Temperature Control

Another advantage of gas grills is the ability to precisely control the temperature. In contrast to traditional charcoal grills, which can be difficult to operate, gas grills allow you to precisely change the temperature, providing you greater control over the cooking process. This precise temperature control allows you to cook food more evenly while avoiding overcooking or undercooking. Gas grills also make it simpler to use different heat zones, such as direct and indirect heat, for various cooking techniques.

3. adaptability

Gas grills are also quite adaptable. They may be used to cook everything from traditional burgers and hot dogs to delicate fish and veggies. Furthermore, gas grills can be used for a variety of cooking methods such as grilling, smoking, roasting, and baking. Because of this adaptability, gas grills are an excellent choice for outdoor cooking aficionados who prefer to try new foods and cooking methods.

4. Healthier Cooking

Gas grilling is a cleaner cooking method than other outdoor cooking methods such as charcoal grilling or smoking. Gas grills produce less smoke and soot, resulting in less cleanup after cooking. Furthermore, gas grills allow excess fat to drain off the meal, lowering overall fat content and making it a healthier cooking option.

5. Saves time

Gas grills are also an efficient way to cook. They heat up quickly and cook food faster than other techniques of outdoor cooking. This means you'll be able to spend less time cooking and more time enjoying your meal and company. Furthermore, gas grills allow you to prepare many foods at once, which can save you even more time.

6. It is safe and simple to use.

Finally, gas grills are both safe and simple to operate. They eliminate the need for open flames, potentially lowering the risk of fires. Furthermore, gas grills are simple to start, operate, and clean, making them a convenient cooking alternative. Many gas grills also include safety features like automatic shut-off valves, making them even safer to operate.

Finally, cooking on a gas grill offers several benefits and characteristics that make it a great choice for outdoor meals. Gas grills are practical, precise, adaptable, clean, time-saving, safe, and simple to operate. A gas grill is a versatile and efficient cooking choice that can help you produce tasty and nutritious meals for your friends and family, whether you're preparing for a huge family gathering or just grilling up a quick midweek supper.

Tips and Tricks for Preparing and Using the Gas Grill:

Grilling on a gas grill is a great way to cook delicious and flavorful food while enjoying the outdoors. However, to achieve the best results, it's important to prepare and use the gas grill properly. In this section, we will discuss some essential tips and tricks for preparing and using the gas grill, including temperature control, grill placement, and cleaning.

Temperature Control

One of the most important factors in achieving great results on the gas grill is temperature control. Make sure to preheat the grill before cooking, as this will help ensure that your food cooks evenly and retains its moisture. A good rule of thumb is to preheat the grill for at least 10-15 minutes before adding your food.

When it comes to temperature control, it's also important to have a reliable thermometer. Some gas grills come with built-in thermometers, but if yours doesn't, consider investing in an infrared thermometer to accurately measure the temperature of the grill grates. This will help you cook your food to perfection, whether you're searing a steak or grilling delicate seafood.

Grill Placement

Another key factor in successful gas grilling is grill placement. It's important to place your food on the grill grates in the right location, depending on what you're cooking. For example, thicker cuts of meat should be placed over indirect heat, while thinner cuts can be cooked over direct heat.

It's also important to keep your grill grates clean and well-oiled to prevent food from sticking. Before cooking, use a stiff wire brush to scrape off any debris or residue from the grates. Then, use a paper towel or brush to apply a light layer of oil to the grates to help prevent sticking.

Cleaning

Proper cleaning is crucial for maintaining the performance and longevity of your gas grill. Make sure to clean your grill after each use, using a wire brush to scrape off any debris or residue from the grates. Then, use a damp cloth or sponge to wipe down the exterior of the grill, including the lid, sides, and base.

It's also important to clean the grease trap and burner tubes periodically, as these can become clogged with grease and other debris over time. Refer to your grill's manual for specific instructions on how to clean these components.

Gas Safety

Gas grills are generally safe to use, but it's important to take certain precautions to prevent accidents. Make sure to always turn off the gas supply and the burners after use, and never leave the grill unattended while it's in use. If you smell gas or notice any other signs of a gas leak, turn off the gas supply immediately and contact a professional for assistance.

Accessories

Finally, consider investing in some accessories to make your gas grilling experience even better. A good set of grilling tools, including tongs, spatulas, and a meat thermometer, can help you cook your food to perfection. Other accessories, such as grill covers, drip pans, and smoker boxes, can also enhance your grilling experience and help you achieve great results.

In conclusion, preparing and using a gas grill requires a few key tips and tricks to achieve the best results. Temperature control, grill placement, and cleaning are essential factors in successful gas grilling. Gas safety is also important to prevent accidents, and investing in accessories can enhance your grilling experience. By following these tips and tricks, you can enjoy delicious and flavorful food cooked to perfection on your gas grill.

Cleaning the Grill:

Cleaning your gas grill properly is critical to its performance and lifetime. A clean grill not only looks nicer, but it also cooks better and aids in the prevention of flare-ups and other safety issues. This section will go over 15 cleaning recommendations for your gas barbecue, including both daily and periodic cleaning duties.

Brush the Grill Grates

The grill grates are one of the most crucial parts of your gas barbecue to clean. Scrape any trash or residue from the grates with a strong wire brush before and after each usage. For severe filth, use a grill grate cleaner or a baking soda and water mixture.

Soak the grill grates in water

If your grill grates are particularly unclean or oily, soak them for 30 minutes to an hour in warm soapy water before cleaning them clean. This can assist in softening the filth and making it easier to remove.

Make use of a Drip Pan.

A drip pan behind the barbecue grates can assist capture grease and other debris, making cleanup easier after grilling. After each usage, make sure to empty and clean the drip pan.

ean the Burner Tubes of Grease and Debris.

her vital component to clean on your gas grill is the burner tubes. Remove the grates and heat
, then clean any dirt or grease from the burner tubes using a wire brush or a grill brush.

ilds Should Be Cleaned

eat shields can become clogged with grease and debris, affecting the effectiveness of your
the heat shields and clean them with a grill cleaner or warm soapy water.

an electronic igniter, make sure to clean it on a regular basis to guarantee optimal
ny trash or residue from the igniter with a toothbrush or a wire brush.

ir

lso become dirty with time. To maintain the grill looking its best, wash clean
a damp cloth or sponge on a regular basis.

Another vital component to clean on your gas grill is the grease trap. After each usage, empty the grease trap and clean it with warm soapy water or a grill cleaner.

Make use of a Cover

Using a grill cover can help protect your grill from the elements and keep dirt and debris off the outside. Make care to clean the cover on a regular basis.

Wash the Grill Brush

Over time, the grill brush might become filthy and greasy. Clean it with warm soapy water on a regular basis, or replace it if it becomes too worn or torn.

Make Use of a Non-Toxic Cleaner

Use a non-toxic cleaner to clean your gas grill so that no dangerous residue is left on your food or in the environment.

Wear Safety Equipment

Cleaning your gas barbecue can be a difficult and time-consuming task. Wear protective gloves and eye protection to avoid injuries and stay clean.

Make use of a Power Washer.

Consider using a power washer to clean the grill grates and other components if the filth is tough or the grill is large. To avoid harming the grill, use a lower pressure setting.

Clean on a regular basis

Regular cleaning is essential for keeping a clean and functional gas barbecue. Make it a practice to clean your grill after each usage and to do deep cleanings on a regular basis during the grilling season.

Professional Maintenance Should Be Scheduled

If you are not comfortable performing gas grill maintenance on your own, consider hiring a professional. A certified technician may inspect and clean your grill to verify it is working properly.

Recommended accessories and equipment

Using the appropriate accessories and equipment can improve and enhance your grilling experience. In this section, we will go over some of the best gas barbecue accessories and equipment.

Grilling Brush

A decent grill brush is crucial for cleaning the grates of your grill before and after use. Look for a brush with strong bristles and a long handle for ease of use.

Thermometer for Meat

A meat thermometer is an essential tool for ensuring that your meal is cooked to the proper temperature. For accurate temperature readings, look for a thermometer with a digital readout and a long probe.

Grill Shield

A grill cover is an essential piece of equipment for protecting your gas grill from the elements and extending its life. Look for a cover that is made of durable materials and fits snuggly over your grill.

Gloves for grilling

Grilling gloves can shield your hands from heat and help you avoid burns when working with hot grates and food. Look for gloves that are resistant to heat and have a solid grip.

Set of Grilling Tools

A grilling tool set, which commonly comprises a spatula, tongs, and a fork, can make handling food on the grill easier. Look for a package that includes solid and long-lasting grilling equipment.

Griddle Basket

A grilling basket is an excellent addition for grilling smaller things like veggies or shrimp that could otherwise fall through the barbecue grates. Look for a basket with a long handle and nonstick materials for easy mobility.

Chips or pellets of wood

Wood chips or pellets added to your gas barbecue can enhance the flavor and scent of your cuisine. Look for wood chips or pellets made of high-quality materials that are suitable with your gas barbecue.

Grilling Light

A grill light can make grilling easier in low-light situations, such as at night. Choose a light that is simple to install and has a bright, adjustable beam.

Grilling Mat

A barbecue mat can help keep food off the grates and make cleanup easier. Look for a mat made of nonstick materials that is intended for use with gas grills.

Thermocouple Infrared Thermometer

An infrared thermometer can help you determine whether the surface temperature of your grill grates is hot enough to start cooking. Look for an infrared thermometer with a broad temperature range and a sturdy construction.

Rotisserie grill

A grill rotisserie can help you roast larger portions of meat evenly and crispy on the outside. Look for a rotisserie that fits your gas grill and has a robust motor for smooth, steady rotation.

Box for Smoking

A smoker box can be used to provide a smokey flavor to your meal without using a regular smoker. Look for a smoker box built of robust materials that is simple to install and use.

Griddle Pan

A griddle plate can be used on your gas grill to cook pancakes, eggs, and other breakfast items. Look for a griddle plate constructed of nonstick materials that is simple to clean.

Pizza Oven

A pizza stone may be used on your gas barbecue to cook wonderful pizzas. Choose a pizza stone constructed of high-quality materials and intended for use with gas grills.

Ice chest or cooler

While barbecuing outside, a cooler or ice chest can be utilized to keep your drinks and food cold. Look for a cooler that is portable and has a high capacity.

Finally, employing the correct accessories and equipment can improve and enhance your grilling experience. As a result, search for high-quality accessories and equipment made for use with gas barbecues.

Breakfast and Brunch

1. Cornmeal pancakes

Portion Size: 2
Duration: 45 minutes

Ingredients:

3/4 cup of cornmeal
5/8 cups of flour
1/4 tsp of baking soda and 1/2 teaspoon of salt.
One cup of buttermilk
One egg
2 tbsp butter or 4 tbsp margarine

Instructions:

In a mixing bowl, combine the salt, cornmeal, baking soda, and salt. Add the buttermilk and eggs (or, if not using buttermilk, combine the milk and vinegar first, then whisk in the eggs). Whisk together the wet, dry, and melted ingredients.
Pour batter into a lightly oiled baking dish. Flip when surface bubbles appear. On the side, drizzle with normal or maple syrup.

Nutrition Facts (1 portion):

Energy: 472 Kcal
Carbs: 61g
Proteins: 15g
Fats: 19g

2. Denver Omelet Salad

Portion Size: 2
Duration: 25 minutes

Ingredients:

four cups of a fresh baby spinach
a half-cup of chopped tomatoes
One tablespoon of olive oil
1 cup ham, cooked and chopped
one small onion, and one tiny green pepper, diced
two big eggs
Pepper and Salt to your liking

Instructions:
Set aside the spinach and tomatoes in a bowl. In a large skillet, heat a single tablespoon of olive oil over medium-high heat. Cook for about 7 minutes, or until the ham is fully heated through, with the onion and green pepper. Top with tomatoes and spinach. Warm the remaining oil in the same skillet. Crack one egg into a small cup, then carefully slide it into the pan. Sprinkle with salt and pepper and remove from heat immediately. Cooking sunny-side-up eggs in a covered pan until done. Toss the salad with fried eggs.

Nutrition Facts (1 portion):

Energy: 229 Kcal
Carbs: 7 g
Proteins: 20 g
Fats: 14g

3. Apple Cinnamon Overnight Oats

Portion Size: 2
Duration: 5 min

Ingredients:

Traditional oats, 1 cup
One sliced medium-sized Gala / Honeycrisp apple
2 tbsp. raisins
two cups of Milk that is 2%
1/8 of a tsp of cinnamon powder
a pinch of salt
Optional: roasted diced nuts

Instructions:

Put together the Materials in little bottle. Overnight refrigeration is recommended after sealing.

Nutrition Facts (1 portion):

Energy: 349 Kcal
Carbs: 59 g
Proteins:14 g
Fats: 8 g

4. S'mores Waffle Sandwich

Portion Size: 2
Duration: Ten minutes

Ingredients:

One frozen waffle
Half a bar of candy (milk chocolate), pieced
Quarter cup of miniature marshmallow

Instructions:

Waffles should be crisped up on the grill for around 4 minutes.
Place half of a milk chocolate candy bar and marshmallows on top of one waffle.
Wrap the remaining waffle in it.
until the chocolate melts, grill for about a minute.

Nutrition Facts (1 serving):

Energy: 62 Kcal
Carbs: 9.29 g
Proteins:1.21 g
Fats: 2.28 g

5. Chia Pudding

Portion Size: 2
Duration: 10 min

Ingredients:

One-fourth cup of entire white chia seeds
One cup of milk (soy/ almond)
Vanilla extract, 1 tsp
1 banana
2 -3 dates, pitted
3 dashes cinnamon

Instructions:

Add chia seeds to the bowl. Add vanilla essence to the milk that has been poured on top.
Stir thoroughly.
Let the bowl rest for ten mins while stirring regularly.
Place for a minimum of four hours (overnight is acceptable) in the refrigerator.

Nutrition Facts (1 portion):

Energy: 224Kcal
Carbs: 36g
Proteins: 6g
Fats: 8g

6. Grilled Chicken Pita

Portion Size: 2
Duration: half an hour
Ingredients:
half lb. Chicken Thighs (skinless and boneless)
0.5 cup Lemon & Garlic Marinade
Pepper and salt as desired
half tsp Pure Oil (olive)
half lb. Organic Hearty Grain Pita, divided
4Tbsp Tzatziki Dip, divided
1plum tomato, cored, 1/2-inch dice, or 4 Cherry Tomatoes, quartered
1/4 onion, diced
half cucumber, peeled, halved lengthwise, seeds removed, 1/4-inch dice
Optional: Plain Crumbled Feta Cheese, as desired
Instructions:
Combine the chicken and marinade. Refrigerate for 12-24 hours while marinating in the refrigerator. For 10 minutes, preheat the grill to HIGH. Chicken should be salted and peppered, with a small spray of oil on each side. Cover the chicken and place it on the grill. Reduce the heat to MED-HIGH. Cook for 9-10 minutes at 155°F. Remove it off the grill. Allow it to settle for about 2 minutes at 165 degrees. Cut the chicken into slices. After about a minute of grilling or microwaving, pitas should be warm and flexible. 2 tablespoons tzatziki should be spread across the middle of each entire pita. On top, evenly distribute the chicken, red onion, cucumber, and tomatoes. If preferred, top each pita with feta cheese crumbles.

Nutrition Facts (1 portion):
Energy: 560Kcal

11. Ham & Brie Croissant Sandwich

Portion Size: 2
Duration: 10 minutes

Ingredients:

2 Tbsp Organic Mayonnaise
2 tsp Organic Spicy Brown Mustard or your favorite mustard
1/2 pkg (2 pack) Large Plain Croissants, sliced
1/8 lb. Mild Brie (Cheese Shop), sliced, divided
4 slices Ham divided

Instructions:

Combine mustard with mayonnaise in a pot. Each sliced croissant should have a mayonnaise mixture distributed evenly over the bottom half.
Two slices of ham are added after the brie slices, on an even basis.
Add the remaining croissant halves on top.

Nutrition Facts (1 portion):

Energy: 520Kcal
Carbs: 24g
Proteins: 16g
Fats: 39g

12. Summer Fruit Trifle

Portion Size: 2
Duration: 15 min

Ingredients:

1/8 Angel Food Cake Ring, cut into 1-inch pieces (about 15 pieces)
quarter cup brewed Coffee, cooled
1/2 cup Vanilla Low fat Yogurt
One cup fresh berry
half plum, pitted, sliced
2 tbsp of Grape-Nuts Cereal

Instructions:

On a baking sheet, arrange the cake pieces. Drizzle the coffee over them, rotating them to coat all sides.
Layer cake, yogurt, berries, plums, and cereal in a 2-quart serving bowl or two glasses, reserving some yogurt and fruit for decoration.
Let relax for 10 min in the freezer.

Nutrition Facts (1 portion):

Energy: 190 Kcal
Carbs: 42g
Proteins: 6g
Fats: 3g

5. Chia Pudding

Portion Size: 2
Duration: 10 min

Ingredients:

One-fourth cup of entire white chia seeds
One cup of milk (soy/ almond)
Vanilla extract, 1 tsp
1 banana
2 -3 dates, pitted
3 dashes cinnamon

Instructions:

Add chia seeds to the bowl. Add vanilla essence to the milk that has been poured on top.
Stir thoroughly.
Let the bowl rest for ten mins while stirring regularly.
Place for a minimum of four hours (overnight is acceptable) in the refrigerator.

Nutrition Facts (1 portion):

Energy: 224Kcal
Carbs: 36g
Proteins: 6g
Fats: 8g

6. Grilled Chicken Pita

Portion Size: 2
Duration: half an hour
Ingredients:
half lb. Chicken Thighs (skinless and boneless)
0.5 cup Lemon & Garlic Marinade
Pepper and salt as desired
half tsp Pure Oil (olive)
half lb. Organic Hearty Grain Pita, divided
4Tbsp Tzatziki Dip, divided
1plum tomato, cored, 1/2-inch dice, or 4 Cherry Tomatoes, quartered
1/4 onion, diced
half cucumber, peeled, halved lengthwise, seeds removed, 1/4-inch dice
Optional: Plain Crumbled Feta Cheese, as desired
Instructions:
Combine the chicken and marinade. Refrigerate for 12-24 hours while marinating in the refrigerator. For 10 minutes, preheat the grill to HIGH. Chicken should be salted and peppered, with a small spray of oil on each side. Cover the chicken and place it on the grill. Reduce the heat to MED-HIGH. Cook for 9-10 minutes at 155°F. Remove it off the grill. Allow it to settle for about 2 minutes at 165 degrees. Cut the chicken into slices. After about a minute of grilling or microwaving, pitas should be warm and flexible. 2 tablespoons tzatziki should be spread across the middle of each entire pita. On top, evenly distribute the chicken, red onion, cucumber, and tomatoes. If preferred, top each pita with feta cheese crumbles.

Nutrition Facts (1 portion):
Energy: 560Kcal

Carbs: 46g
Proteins: 34g
Fats: 30g

Fats: 7 g

7. Savory Hot Cereal with Apple

Portion Size: 2
Duration: 15 minutes

Ingredients:

1 medium-size Ginger Gold or Granny Smith apples
One and a half cups of water
half tablespoon Basting Oil
2.5 packets (1 oz each) instant cream of wheat cereal
1/4 cup Italian Classics Grated Grana Padano Cheese
Pepper
Salt

Instructions:

Grate and slice one apple thinly.
Grated apples, water, and basting oil are put in a container and boiled.
Put cheese with cream of wheat in a dish. Put the apple-water combination and combine for a minute to thicken.
Incorporate pepper and salt as desired.
Pour into warmed-up dishes and top with apple slices.

Nutrition Facts (1 portion):

Energy: 260 Kcal
Carbs: 40 g
Proteins: 8 g

8. Strawberry-Cherry Smoothie

Portion Size: 2
Duration: 5 minutes

Ingredients:

half cup Strawberry Probiotic Kefir
half a cup Dark Sweet Cherries

Instructions:

In a blender, combine cherries and kefir.
Add protein powder if desired. Until smooth, blend.
Chef's advice: You can substitute any frozen fruit for cherries.

Nutrition Facts (1 portion):

Energy: 120 Kcal
Carbs: 23 g
Proteins: 6 g
Fats: 1 g

9. Simple Scrambled Eggs

Portion Size: 2
Duration: 15 minutes

Ingredients:

4 Large Eggs
4 Tbsp 2% Reduced Fat Milk
Pepper and salt as desired
Cooking Spray

Instructions:

Whisk together the eggs, milk, and salt; reserve.
Spray cooking spray on a small nonstick pan and heat it on MED.
The eggs will continue to cook once plated. Spread the pan with the egg mixture. Cook, stirring constantly with a spatula, for 3–4 mins. Incorporate pepper with salt, transfer to a plate.

Nutrition Facts (1 portion):

Energy: 160Kcal
Carbs: 2g
Proteins: 13g
Fats: 11 g

10. Roasted Mango with Vanilla Yogurt

Portion Size: 2
Duration: 15 minutes

Ingredients:

One mango
1 tablespoon of Oil (olive)
2 tablespoons of Organic Pure Cane Light Brown Sugar
Pepper to taste
2 Tbsp Vanilla Low-fat Yogurt
1 1/2 Tbsp thinly sliced Mint

Instructions:

SET oven to BROIL. Slice the unpeeled mango's wide sides away from the pit. Cut meat into cubes, then gently invert the cubes to separate them. Put the mango halves in a shallow casserole tray. Sprinkle it with brown sugar and add oil and pepper.
Roast for 3 to 5 minutes on highest oven shelf. Add yogurt on top, then add mint as a garnish.

Nutrition Facts (1 Portion):

Energy: 250 Kcal
Carbs: 50 g
Proteins: 3 g
Fats: 7 g

11. Ham & Brie Croissant Sandwich

Portion Size: 2
Duration: 10 minutes

Ingredients:

2 Tbsp Organic Mayonnaise
2 tsp Organic Spicy Brown Mustard or your favorite mustard
1/2 pkg (2 pack) Large Plain Croissants, sliced
1/8 lb. Mild Brie (Cheese Shop), sliced, divided
4 slices Ham divided

Instructions:

Combine mustard with mayonnaise in a pot. Each sliced croissant should have a mayonnaise mixture distributed evenly over the bottom half.
Two slices of ham are added after the brie slices, on an even basis.
Add the remaining croissant halves on top.

Nutrition Facts (1 portion):

Energy: 520Kcal
Carbs: 24g
Proteins: 16g
Fats: 39g

12. Summer Fruit Trifle

Portion Size: 2
Duration: 15 min

Ingredients:

1/8 Angel Food Cake Ring, cut into 1-inch pieces (about 15 pieces)
quarter cup brewed Coffee, cooled
1/2 cup Vanilla Low fat Yogurt
One cup fresh berry
half plum, pitted, sliced
2 tbsp of Grape-Nuts Cereal

Instructions:

On a baking sheet, arrange the cake pieces. Drizzle the coffee over them, rotating them to coat all sides.
Layer cake, yogurt, berries, plums, and cereal in a 2-quart serving bowl or two glasses, reserving some yogurt and fruit for decoration.
Let relax for 10 min in the freezer.

Nutrition Facts (1 portion):

Energy: 190 Kcal
Carbs: 42g
Proteins: 6g
Fats: 3g

13. Roasted Asparagus with Parmigiano-Reggiano

Portion Size: 2
Duration: 20 minutes

Ingredients:

One lb. of trimmed asparagus
Two Tablespoons Wegmans Olive Oil
Two Tablespoon Italian Classics Grated Parmigiano Reggiano
Pepper
Salt

Instructions:

Set the oven temperature to 400.
Combine oil with asparagus in a pot.
Place a layer on a baking tray and roast for about 15 mins or until tender and gently browned.
Take out of the oven.
Cheese should be distributed evenly after liberally seasoning using pepper and salt.
Roast again for 5 mins to soften the cheese.

Nutrition Facts (1 portion):

Energy: 130Kcal
Carbs: 4g
Proteins: 4g
Fats: 12g

14. Crunchy French Toast

Portion Size: 2
Duration: 20 minutes

Ingredients:

Three big eggs
57-gram fat-free milk
Vanilla extract, 1 tsp
1/4 tsp of salt
Crushed half a cup of frosted cornflakes
0.5 cup old-fashioned oats
1/2cup sliced almonds
4 slices whole wheat bread
Maple syrup

Instructions:

Mix the salt, milk, vanilla, and eggs in container. Combine cornflakes, oats, as well as almonds in another container. Cooking spray-coated griddle heated to medium heat. Coat bread in egg and then cereal mix from both sides. Using a griddle, toast it on both sides for 3 mins. Serve topped with syrup.

Nutrition Facts (1 portion):

Energy: 335 Kcal
Carbs: 43g
Proteins: 17 g
Fats: 11 g

15. Sweet Potato and Egg Skillet

Portion Size: 2
Duration: 25 min

Ingredients:

One tablespoon of butter
a medium-sized sweet potato, peeled and sliced
half chopped garlic
Salt, one pinch
A quarter of a teaspoon of dry thyme
one cup of fresh baby spinach
two big eggs
a quarter of a teaspoon of finely ground pepper

Instructions:

In a big pot, carefully melt the butter. Cook, covered, for about 5 minutes, or until potatoes are almost done. Sweet potatoes, thyme, salt, and garlic are added. Cook for two minutes after adding the spinach. By spoon, four wells should have been created in the potato mixture. Add an egg to each well. In eggs, season with ground pepper and the remaining quarter teaspoon salt. Cook, covered, until the yolks begin to thicken but remain soft.

Nutrition Facts (1 portion):

Energy: 224 Kcal
Carbs: 24 g
Proteins: 8 g
Fats: 11 g

16. Waffle Breakfast Sandwich

Portion Size: 2
Duration: 12 minutes

Ingredients:

half waffles
a quarter of an egg, scrambled
A quarter of a slice of cheese
1/2 slices ham (any lunch meat will do)
butter syrup (optional)

Instructions:

Spoon egg scrambled onto waffles, covering all of the groves.
Cook for about 10 mins on a well-greased pan. until the waffles are gently toasted and the eggs are done.
Choose cheese and ham for your sandwich's base.
If desired, drizzle some warm syrup over top.

Nutrition Facts (1 portion):

Energy: 25Kcal
Carbs: 0.26g
Proteins: 1.6g
Fats: 1.94g

17. Hash Brown & Egg Bake

Portion Size: 2
Duration: 45 min

Ingredients:

8 oz hash brown potatoes, thawed
4 slices turkey bacon
2 eggs and a quarter-cup of grated cheddar cheese
a half-cup of low-fat milk
2 green onions, chopped
paprika sprinkled on top

Instructions:

Eggs and milk should be thoroughly beaten. Add the bacon, hash browns, onion, pepper, and half of the cheese.
Pam-spray a pan that is 8 inches square.
Add paprika after pouring the mixture into the pan.
On top, sprinkle the remaining cheese. Bake uncovered at 350 degrees for 45 mins.

Nutrition Facts (1 portion):

Energy: 285 Kcal
Carbs: 17 g
Proteins: 20 g
Fats: 15 g

18. Potato Frittata

Portion Size: 2
Duration: 20 min

Ingredients:

1 tablespoon olive oil
1 cup of yellow onions, peeled and chopped
1/2 pound. diced, peeled baking potatoes
pepper, and salt as desired
1.5 tablespoons of whipped butter
4 large, gently whisked brown eggs
1 tablespoon freshly trimmed chives
Organic Cilantro, cut to a half-tbsp.
a quarter of an 8-ounce package of The Little Fireworks Blend of Shredded Pizza Cheese
A quarter cup of warmed Gold's Extra Chunky Salsa

Instructions:

The oil should be heated until it begins to smoke. Add the onions and cook for two to three minutes. Cook for 10 minutes, or until the potatoes are golden on both sides. Season with pepper and salt to taste. Add the butter. Gradually add the eggs, whisking them in with a rubber spatula as the butter melts. Cook for 2-3 minutes, stirring occasionally, or until nearly done. Combine cilantro and chives. After uniformly distributing the potato-egg mixture on the bottom of the pan, sprinkle with cheese. Cut into 2 wedges and serve with salsa.

Nutrition Facts (1 portion):

Energy: 480Kcal
Carbs: 30g

Proteins: 22g
Fats: 29g

19. Mango on Multigrain Toast

Portion Size: 2
Duration: 10 min

Ingredients:

1/2 mango, peeled, sliced
1/2Tbsp Organic Pure Maple Syrup
2 slices Multigrain Bread, toasted
2 oz Camembert soft-ripened cheese, cut in 2 thin slices
Freshly ground pepper to taste

Instructions:

Mango and syrup should be combined in a small basin and mixed together.
A single slab of cheese, 1/4 of the mango, and pepper are placed on the toast as the toppings.

Nutrition Facts (1 portion):

Energy: 280Kcal
Carbs: 43g
Proteins: 10g
Fats: 7g

20. Breakfast Burritos

Portion Size: 2
Duration: 10 min

Ingredients:

2 Large Eggs
2 8-inch Gordita Style Fajita Tortillas
A quarter of five ounces Baby Spinach
A quarter cup fancy Mexican shredded Cheese
Organic Olive Cooking Spray
2Tbsp Mild Salsa, divided
Pepper, salt, as desired

Instructions:

Set aside the eggs after combining them. Heat a big nonstick skillet to MED-HIGH. On both sides, place one tortilla on a dry griddle and quickly heat and stretch it for 15 seconds. Cover and place on platter. Repeat, stacking the tortillas to keep them warm. Spray the pan with cooking spray. After dumping the eggs, add the cheese and spinach. Cook for 1-1 1/2 minutes, stirring frequently, or until the eggs are set and the spinach has wilted. Season with pepper and salt to taste. Spread an even amount of egg mixture in the center of each tortilla, leaving two inches around the sides. To each, add 1 tablespoon salsa. Fold the top and bottom edges of the tortilla halfway around the filling. Continue rolling the tortilla over to make a tight burrito.

Nutrition Facts (1 portion):

Energy: 270 Kcal
Carbs: 28 g
Proteins: 14 g

Fats: 12 g

21. Egg & Cheese Bagel Sandwich

Portion Size: 2
Duration: 15 minutes

Ingredients:

Two Plain Bagel toasted
Olive Oil Cooking Spray
2 Large Egg
Pepper, salt, as desired
Two slices Yellow American Cheese Singles

Instructions:

Heat a nonstick pan on MEDIUM after misting it using oil spray. Gently put the eggs and add salt with pepper in it.
Cook eggs covered for 3–4 mins, or till the yolk is the desired doneness with the whites completely set.
Cheese, egg, and toasted bagel bottom half are layered on top of each other.
Quickly serve.

Nutrition Facts (1 portion):

Energy: 420 Kcal
Carbs: 64 g
Proteins: 19 g
Fats: 11 g

22. Easy Egg Drop Soup

Portion Size: 2
Duration: 20 min

Ingredients:

Two cups of water
4 tsp Vegetarian Chicken less Broth Concentrate
1/2 Large Egg
1/2 bunch fresh chives, trimmed, minced
Pepper, salt, as desired

Instructions:

Put water in the pot to bring it a boil.
To boiling water, add egg and broth concentration.
Whisk quickly for 1 minute to fry the egg.
Salt and pepper as desired; add chives.

Nutrition Facts (1 portion):

Energy: 45Kcal
Carbs: 4g
Proteins: 2g
Fats: 3g

24. Avocado Toast with Soft-Boiled Egg

Portion Size: 2
Duration: 15 min

Ingredients:

2 slices Organic Sprouted Multigrain Sandwich Bread, toasted
1 Avocado, pitted, peeled, smashed
2 Organic Large Brown Eggs, soft-boiled, peeled, sliced
To your liking, use hot habanero pepper sauce.
Pepper and salt as desired

Instructions:

Avocado should be evenly spread on bread before egg slices are added. Add salt, sauce as well as pepper as per preference.

Nutrition Facts (1 portion):

Energy: 330 Kcal
Carbs: 26 g
Proteins: 12 g
Fats: 20 g

25. Peach Gazpacho

Portion Size: 2
Duration: 10 min

Ingredients:

half a cup sliced peaches, frozen
half cup of roughly chopped pineapple
half cup of Orange Juice
A quarter cup of White Granulated Sugar
Juice of half lime
3 oz Vanilla Low-fat Yogurt
1/2tsp chopped Organic Mint

Instructions:

Put 4 slices of peach aside.
Blend the remaining peaches, pineapple, sugar, lime juice, and orange juice for 2 minutes or until smooth.
Put yogurt, the peach slices you saved, and the minced mint.

Nutrition Facts (1 portion):

Energy: 200Kcal
Carbs: 49 g
Proteins: 2 g
Fats: 1 g

Appetizers and Side Dishes

1. Guacamole

Portion Size: 2
Duration: 15 minutes

Ingredients:

1/8 of a finely sliced red onion
Juice of 1 lime
3 avocados, pitted
1 1/2 tsp Tabasco Pepper Sauce
Cilantro, cut into 2 Tbsps.
Salt, according to preference

Instructions:

In a blender, puree the onion and lime juice; reserve. Add the avocado to the container and crush it using a spoon to make it lumpy.
Add cilantro, Tabasco, and the onion-lime combination to the avocado. Add salt and stir thoroughly.

Nutrition Facts (1 portion):

Energy: 35 Kcal
Carbs: 2 g
Proteins: 0 g
Fats: 3 g

2. Classic Deviled Eggs

Portion Size: 2
Duration: 10 minutes

Ingredients:

1 hard-boiled egg, halved
2 tbsp of mayonnaise
1/6 tsp rice wine vinegar
1/2 tsp dill, chopped
1/6 tsp Dijon mustard
1/10 tsp garlic powder
1/10 tsp salt
2 sprigs fresh dill (optional)

Instructions:

Put egg with water in a pot. Boil on high heat. Cook for 12 minutes on low heat.
Place egg whites aside and scoop egg yolks into a basin. Egg yolks, Dijon mustard, garlic powder, salt, 1/2 tsp minced dill, mayonnaise, and vinegar are mashed together.
Fill egg whites with yolk mixture. Add dill sprigs as a garnish. Refrigerate until serving.

Nutrition Facts (1 portion):

Energy: 76.84Kcal
Carbs: 0.36g
Proteins: 3.3g
Fats: 6.91g

3. Fried Cabbage

Portion Size: 2
Duration: 20 minutes

Ingredients:

1/2 Tbsp butter
1/4 tsp of sugar
1/8 tsp of salt
1/8 tsp of pepper flakes
1/10 tsp of ground pepper
2 cups coarsely chopped cabbage
1/4 Tbsp water

Instructions:

Take a pan and melt butter in it.
Put pepper, sugar, salt, and pepper flakes in it.
Combine the water and cabbage in the pot.
While stirring, tender it by cooking for 6 mins.

Nutrition Facts (1 portion):

Energy: 59 Kcal
Carbs: 6 g
Proteins: 1 g
Fats: 4 g

4. Savory Dates

Portion Size: 2
Duration: 15 min

Ingredients:

10 Dried Pitted Dates
1/2 pkg Fresh Goat Cheese, each slice cut in half
10 Dry Roasted Almonds
Sea salt, as desired

Instructions:

Make sure oven is set to 345 degrees.
Place 1 piece of goat cheese inside each date
Add an almond in the center, and sprinkle with sea salt. Put the dates on the baking tray. Roast for 2 mins. Before serving, transfer to a clean dish and chill.

Nutrition Facts (1 portion):

Energy: 150Kcal
Carbs: 27g
Proteins: 3g
Fats: 4g

5. Tropical Fruit Salad

Portion Size: 2
Duration: 15 minutes

Ingredients:

1/3 cup of Sweetened Flaked Coconut
7 oz Mango Chunks
8 oz Pineapple Chunks
Papaya, peeled, seeded, 1-inch dice (about 1 cup)
Juice of 1/2 lime (about 1 Tbsp)
About 10 thinly sliced Mint leaves

Instructions:

On MED, add coconut to a dry pan.
When softly golden-brown, frequently stir for about 5 minutes (watch carefully, it might burn quickly). Using a serving plate, combine the lime juice, pineapple, papaya, mangos, and coconut.
Use mint as a garnish.

Nutrition Facts (1 portion):

Energy: 80 Kcal
Carbs: 16 g
Proteins: 0 g
Fats: 2g

6. Quinoa with Peas and Onion

Portion Size: 2
Duration: 30 min

Ingredients:

3/4 cup of water
1/3 of a cup of washed quinoa
1/3 sliced small onion
1/2 Tbsp olive oil
1/3 of a cup of frozen peas
a pinch of salt
a pinch of pepper
1/3 Tbsp of walnuts, chopped

Instructions:

In a big pot, bring water to a boil. Add the Quinoa and cook for 12 minutes on low heat with the cover on. Remove the quinoa from the heat and fluff it with a fork.
Meanwhile, sauté the onion in oil in a small skillet until tender.
Combine the cooked quinoa with the onions. Add the peas, salt, and pepper and heat well. Sprinkle with walnuts.

Nutrition Facts (1 portion):

Energy: 171 Kcal
Carbs: 24.19 g
Proteins: 6 g
Fats: 5.57g

7. Sweet Corn Dish

Portion Size: 2
Duration: 22 minutes

Ingredients:

3 oz creamed corn
1/4 cup desiccated coconut
1/2 of slightly beaten egg
1/2 tomato

Instructions:

Mix the coconut, egg, and creamed corn together, transfer into an ovenproof dish. Place sliced tomato on top. Place in oven for 20 mins.

Nutrition Facts (1 portion):

Energy: 237 Kcal
Carbs: 23.24 g
Proteins: 4.56 g
Fats: 15.5 g

8. Crispy Baked Onion Rings

Portion Size: 2
Duration: 30 minutes

Ingredients:

1/2 pound of sweet onions
1 1/2 large egg whites
Dry breadcrumbs, 1/2 a cup
1 tsp. thyme powder
1/2 a tsp of paprika
1 tsp of salt
1/8 tsp pepper

Instructions:

Separate onion rings into 1/2-inch rings and place in a bowl. Soak in an ice bath for 30 minutes. Drain.
Egg whites should be foamy.
In a small bowl, combine the bread crumbs, thyme, salt, paprika, and pepper.
Incorporate one-third of the sliced onions into the beaten egg whites, then gradually incorporate the onion rings into the bread crumbs mixture. Coat both sides. Arrange rings on a baking sheet.
Rep with the left mixture.
Cook for 20 minutes, or until crisp and lightly browned. (A temperature of 200 degrees)

Nutrition Facts (1 portion):

Energy: 159Kcal
Carbs: 29g
Proteins: 7g
Fats: 2g

9. Grilled Corn on the Cob

Portion Size: 2
Duration: 15min

Ingredients:

2 ears corn, shucked
1 Tbsp Basting Oil
Salt, as desired

Instructions:

Put the grill on high heat for 10 minutes.
Apply a thin layer of vegetable oil to the cleaned grill grate. Turn heat down to MED.
Sprinkle basting oil over the corn.
Place on the grill then secure the lid. Grill for 8–10 minutes, rotating frequently.
Use salt to season.

Nutrition Facts (1 portion):

Energy: 150 Kcal
Carbs: 19g
Proteins: 3 g
Fats: 8 g

10. Glazed Sweet Potatoes

Portion Size: 2
Duration: 60 minutes

Ingredients:

1/2 lb. sweet potatoes
1/10 cup butter, cubed
1/10 cup maple syrup
2 tbsp of brown sugar
1/10 tsp of ground cinnamon

Instructions:

Put fresh sweet potatoes and water in a big pot. Boil, lower the heat, and then simmer for 35 mins.
Rinse, let it cool a bit then peel and slice into pieces and put in a 2-qt baking dish.
Set the oven to 350°F.
Combine butter, syrup, brown sugar, and cinnamon in a small pot and bring to boil while being constantly stirred.
Add to the potatoes.
Bake without cover for 30 to 40 mins.

Nutrition Facts (1 portion):

Energy: 200Kcal
Carbs: 36 g
Proteins: 2.34 g
Fats: 5.75 g

11. Hummus

Portion Size: 2
Duration: 10 min

Ingredients:

14 oz of chickpeas
1/8 of a cup of sesame paste (tahini)
1/6 of a cup of lemon juice
1/2 tsp of salt
1/3 of a garlic clove
3/4 cup of the reserved liquid
1/10 tsp Cumin
2/3 Tbsps. finely chopped parsley
2 Tbsps. of olive oil

Instructions:

Drain chickpeas and set liquid aside.
Chop and peel the garlic.
To make a thick paste, combine the chickpeas, garlic, tahini, lemon juice, and salt in a food blender. Add tahini, salt, and lemon juice till the mixture tastes right to you.
If it is too dry, gradually add (tsp) of the conserved liquid.
Eat with crackers, pita, or Arabic bread, and top with parsley and olive oil.

Nutrition Facts (1 portion):

Energy: 209 Kcal
Carbs: 18 g
Proteins: 6.4 g
Fats: 13.37 g

12. Apple Chips

Portion Size: 2
Duration: 1 Hour 10 min

Ingredients:

1/2 of Granulated Cane Sugar
1/2 of water
1/2 tsp vanilla beans
1/2 sliced apple

Instructions:

Preheat the oven to 225 degrees Fahrenheit.
Combine the sugar, water, and vanilla beans in a saucepan. Bring to a boil, then reduce to a simmer for about 2 minutes.
Allow to cool after removing from the heat.
Apple slices are dipped in the cooled sugar mixture and set on a baking sheet lined with parchment paper.
Bake the apples for 50-60 minutes in the center of the oven, or until they begin to turn light golden.
Remove and set aside for one minute to crisp.

Nutrition Facts (1 portion):

Energy: 80Kcal
Carbs: 21g
Proteins: 0g
Fats: 0g

13. Smoked Salmon Pinwheels

Portion Size: 2
Duration: 10min

Ingredients:

7/10 oz pack (approx.) of smoked salmon slices
9/10 oz cream cheese softened
1/5 tsp lemon pepper seasoning
1/5 tbsp finely chopped parsley

Instructions:

Combine soft cream cheese, parsley, lemon pepper spice, and a touch of salt to spread on toast like butter. Then, add a piece of smoked salmon on top.
Add a second slice on the roll and roll it up tightly until the sandwich is the thickness of a single cucumber.
With a clean knife, cut the pinwheels into small squares, cleaning the blade between each cut, and serve.

Nutrition Facts (1 portion):

Energy: 55 Kcal
Carbs: 0.53 g
Proteins: 2.66 g
Fats: 4.66 g

14. Grilled Peach Salsa

Portion Size: 2
Duration: 30 min

Ingredients:

1 peach, pitted and cut in half.
1 cup Salsa Verde roasted from Wegmans
Juice of 1 lime juice and zest
1 pitted, peeled, and diced avocado
2 tsps. Wegman's Cilantro
Pepper and salt as desired

Instructions:

Turn the grill on HIGH for 10 minutes. Apply a thin layer of vegetable oil to the cleaned grill grate.
Peach should be grilled and cut side down for 3 to 4 minutes or until gently browned. Peel the peach's easily removable skin.
Peach should be diced; then it should be lightly mixed with salsa, lime, avocado, cilantro, and cilantro in a bowl.
 Add salt and pepper as desired.

Nutrition Facts (1 portion):

Energy: 20Kcal
Carbs: 2g
Proteins: 0g
Fats: 2 g

15. Asian Cucumbers

Portion Size: 2
Duration: 1 hour 10 min

Ingredients:

1 cup Seasoned Rice Vinegar
1 organic seedless cucumber, thinly sliced
1 (about 2 oz) shallot, peeled, thinly sliced

Instructions:

On MED-HIGH, bring rice vinegar to a boil. Include in the dish the shallots and cucumbers. Leave at normal temperature for an hour. Serve cold.

Nutrition Facts (1 portion):

Energy: 25Kcal
Carbs: 6g
Proteins: 1g
Fats: 0g

16. Grilled Cauliflower Wedges

Portion Size: 2
Duration: 35 min

Ingredients:

1/3 of a cauliflower
1/6 cup of salted peanuts
1/6 cup shredded strong cheddar cheese
1/6 of a cup of spiced chicken broth

Instructions:

Spread Cauliflower flowerets out on a sizable area of the thick foil.
Add the chicken broth after scattering the peanuts and cheddar cheese.
Place packet with foil sealed inside on grill 6 inches over grey coals.
Turn the package every ten minutes during grilling for 20 to 25 minutes.

Nutrition Facts (1 portion):

Energy: 103 Kcal
Carbs: 6g
Proteins: 6 g
Fats: 7g

17. Chicken Dijon

Portion Size: 2
Duration: 30 min

Ingredients:

3 Tbsps. of butter
6 chicken breasts with the skin and bones
14 oz of chicken broth
1 chopped medium onion
3 Tbsps. Multipurpose flour
3 Tbsps. of Dijon mustard

Instructions:

Using a skillet over medium-high heat, melt the butter. Put the chicken and cook for 2 minutes on both sides or until golden brown. Pour the chicken after whisking the leftover ingredients together. For 20 minutes, simmer with the lid on and the heat on low.

Nutrition Facts (1 portion):

Energy: 528 Kcal
Carbs: 46.5 g
Proteins: 7.88 g
Fats: 36.5 g

18. Brussels Sprouts with Pecans

Portion Size: 2
Duration: 10 min

Ingredients:

1/3 lb. brussels sprouts, halved
1/6 lb. pecan halves
2 tsps. butter
a pinch of salt
a dash of pepper

Instructions:

Brussels sprouts and pecans should be sauteed in butter for 5-7 minutes, or till soft-crisp, in a skillet. Incorporate pepper as well as salt as desired.

Nutrition Facts (1 portion):

Energy: 335 Kcal
Carbs: 12.15g
Proteins: 6.1 g
Fats: 31.8 g

19. Macaroni salad

Portion Size: 2
Duration: 40 min

Ingredients:

1/10 lb. macaroni
1/10 lb. diced celery
1/10 lb. diced cheese
1/10 lb. sweet relish
6 tbsps. chopped onions
salad dressing

Instructions:

Cook macaroni until it is soft.
Drain well, then cool down.
Add onion, cheese, relish, and celery.
To make it delicious and moist, add just enough salad dressing.
To taste, sprinkle on some salt and pepper.

Nutrition Facts (1 portion):

Energy: 145 Kcal
Carbs: 18 g
Proteins: 6.5 g
Fats: 5.26 g

20. Flavorful Green Rice

Portion Size: 2
Duration: 30 min

Ingredients:

1/4 cup finely sliced green onions
2 1/2 tsps. of olive oil
1/8 of a cup of finely chopped parsley
2 1/2 tsp of butter
1/3 of a cup of uncooked rice
1/9 cup Chicken broth
1/10 tsp cayenne pepper
1 bay leaf

Instructions:

Saute onions and parsley in oil and butter for 1 minute, or until they are soft.
Add the rice, stirring occasionally, and cook for 3 minutes, or till transparent and oil-coated.
Bay leaf, pepper, and broth are all stirred up to a boil.
Lessen the heat, cover closely, and simmer for 18 to 20 minutes, or until liquid is absorbed and rice is done.
Get rid of the bay leaf.

Nutrition Facts (1 portion):

Energy: 240Kcal
Carbs: 39g
Proteins: 5g
Fats: 7g

Salads and vegetarian dishes

1. Carrot Salad

Portion Size: 2
Duration: 10 min

Ingredients:

1 1/2 carrots, shredded
1/8 cup peanut butter
1/4 cup of raisins
1 Tbsp of lime juice
1 Tbsp of apple juice
1 tsp of honey

Instructions:

Mix all of the ingredients.

Nutrition Facts (1 portion):

Energy: 190 Kcal
Carbs: 28 g
Proteins: 5 g
Fats: 8 g

2. Vegetable Korma Recipe

Portion Size: 2
Duration: 25 min

Ingredients:
1 Tbsp vegetable oil
1/2 red onion, cut into wedges
1 carrot, peeled and thickly sliced
1/2 cauliflower, cut in florets
1/2 green chili pepper, deseeded and chopped
1 garlic clove, crushed
1/2 Tbsp chopped ginger
1/2 tsp cumin powder
a pinch of coriander powder
1/2 tsp of garam masala
1/3 cup of vegetable stock
a dash of salt
1 1/2 oz of frozen peas
3 tbsp natural yogurt

Instructions:
Heat the oil in a pan over medium heat before adding the onion. Cook for 3-4 minutes, or until the vegetables begin to soften. After adding the carrots, cauliflower, chili, garlic, ginger, and spices, cook for an additional three minutes. Pour in the stock, cover, and cook for 6-7 minutes, or until the potatoes are practically soft. When all of the vegetables are tender, add the peas and continue to cook for another two to three minutes. Turn off the heat and stir in the yogurt once it has thickened. Served with white rice.

Nutrition Facts (1 portion):
Energy: 301Kcal
Carbs: 46g
Proteins: 5g

Fats: 7g

3. Pasta Vegetable Salad

Portion Size: 2
Duration: 15 min

Ingredients:

1/2 cup uncooked tricolor spiral pasta
1/4 broccoli florets
1/2 Cauliflowerets
1/4 of a cup of cucumbers, chopped
1/4 of a cup finely minced celery
1/6 of cup of carrot slices
1/6 of a cup of tomato, chopped
1/8 of a cup of ranch dressing for salad

Instructions:

Cook pasta as directed on the package; drain and rinse under cool water.
Add the veggies and combine in a large bowl. Toss in the salad dressing to coat. Cover and chill for a couple of hours.

Nutrition Facts (1 portion):

Energy: 102 Kcal
Carbs: 62 g
Proteins: 14 g
Fats: 11 g

4. Lemony Chickpeas

Portion Size: 2
Duration: 30 min

Ingredients:

1 cup of instant brown rice, uncooked
1/2 cup olive oil
1 chopped medium onion
1 can of chickpeas, drained, washed
7 Oz from a half-can tomatoes, diced, undrained
1/2 a cup veggie broth
1/8 of a tsp of red pepper flakes
1 1/2 Tbsps. of lemon juice
1/4 of a tsp of grated lemon zest
1/8 of a tsp of pepper

Instructions:

Prepare the rice according to the package directions. While the rice is cooking, heat the oil in a large skillet. Cook until the onion is soft, then add it and stir for 3 to 4 minutes. After adding the chickpeas, tomatoes, broth, pepper, and red pepper flakes, bring to a boil. Simmer at a reduced temperature for ten minutes with the lid on. Boil for 4-5 minutes, stirring occasionally, until the liquid has significantly reduced. Take off the lid. After mixing, add the lemon juice and zest. Serve with rice if desired.

Nutrition Facts (1 portion):

Energy: 433 Kcal
Carbs: 76g
Proteins: 13 g

Fats: 9g

5. Rainbow Hash

Portion Size: 2
Duration: 30 min

Ingredients:

2 tbsp of coconut or olive oil
1 medium-sized purple potato, diced after being peeled
1/2 tsp of dried oregano
1/2 tsp of pepper
1/2 tsp of dried basil
1/2 tsp of sea salt
2 cups of freshly chopped kale or spinach, cut
1 big, peeled, and diced carrot
1 tiny clove of garlic

Instructions:

Heat oil in a big skillet at medium temp. Stir as you cook the potatoes, carrot, and seasonings for 10 to 12 minutes, or until the veggies are soft. Simmer for 2 to 4 minutes after adding the Kale and the garlic.

Nutrition Facts (1 portion):

Energy: 304 Kcal
Carbs: 43g
Proteins: 4g
Fats: 14g

6. Warm Cabbage, Fennel, and Pear Salad

Portion Size: 2
Duration: 25 min

Ingredients:

1 firm medium pear
1 tbsp lemon juice
1 1/2 Tbsps. olive oil
1/2 sliced fennel bulb
2 cups shredded or thinly sliced cabbage
1/8 cup water
1 Tbsp of lemon juice
1 tsp agave nectar
1/2 tsp of kosher salt
1/2 tsp pepper
1/2 cup crumbled or sliced Gorgonzola cheese
1/4 cup chopped walnuts, toasted

Instructions:

After peeling and coring the pears, cut them into 1/2-inch pieces. 1 tbsp lemon juice over the pears to keep their color and freshness. Set the pears aside. Warm the oil in a large wok over a medium-high temperature. Cook for 2-3 minutes, or until the fennel is crisp-tender. Fennel and cabbage should be combined. Cook for another 2-3 minutes, or until both are soft. While gently combining the ingredients, add the pears, water, honey, lemon juice, salt, and pepper to the skillet. Cook for 6–8 minutes, or until the liquid has evaporated. Place on a serving platter. On top, Gorgonzola cheese and roasted walnuts are sprinkled. Serve immediately or at room temperature.

Nutrition Facts (1 portion):
Energy: 391Kcal

Carbs: 28g
Proteins: 9g
Fats: 26g

7. Arugula & Brown Rice Salad

Portion Size: 2
Duration: 25 min

Ingredients:

8.8 oz in half a package prepared-to-serve brown rice
3 cups fresh rocket or young spinach
1 Chickpeas in a half-can, washed and drained
1/2 cup feta cheese crumbles
1/2 cup torn basil leaves, loosely packed
1/4 of a cup of dried cranberry or cherries
dressing:
Olive oil, one eighth of a cup
1 Tbsp of lemon juice
1/8 of a tsp lemon zest
1/8 tsp salt and pepper, each

Instructions:

As directed on the packaging, heat the rice. Place in another big bowl and let it cool a little.
Arugula, beans, cheese, basil, and cherries should all be mixed into the rice.
In a small cup, assemble the dressing's elements.
Over the salad, drizzle; slip into coat.
Serve right away.

Nutrition Facts (1 portion):

Energy: 236 Kcal
Carbs: 26 g
Proteins: 6 g
Fats: 11 g

8. Ginger-Kale Smoothies

Portion Size: 2
Duration: 15 min

Ingredients:

1 cup orange juice
2 cups of freshly torn kale
1/8 of tsp of turmeric powder
4 ice cubes
1 tbsp of fresh ginger root, chopped.
1 tsp of lemon juice
1/8 of a of cinnamon powder
Dash cayenne pepper
1 medium apple, peeled and coarsely chopped
chopped turmeric

Instructions:

Blend the mixture in a blender with the lid on. Pour dispense into chilled glasses, and then serve right away.

Nutrition Facts (1 portion):

Energy: 121Kcal
Carbs: 29 g
Proteins: 1 g
Fats: 0g

9. No-Cook Tomato Sauce

Portion Size: 2
Duration: 10 min
Ingredients:

1 pound (3-4) heirloom tomatoes, halved
2 Tbsp Olive Oil
1/2 tsp of salt

Instructions:

Put a box grater in a big bowl.
Gently rub tomatoes down the medium-sized grater holes, pressing down until all pulp is forced through; discard skins.
Add salt and drizzle with oil.
Serve with bread for dipping.

Nutrition Facts (1 portion):
Energy: 40 Kcal
Carbs: 2g
Proteins: 0g
Fats: 4g

10. Mango Salad with Mint Yogurt Dressing

Portion Size: 2
Duration: 25 min
Ingredients:

1 medium mango, sliced
1/4 unsweetened yogurt
1 medium Gala apple, sliced
1/2 tbsp honey
1/4 of a tsp freshly minced ginger
2 tbsp of lime juice
a pinch of salt
1/8 of a cup of finely cut leaves of fresh mint

Instructions:

Combine mangoes and apples in a sizable bowl.
Add 1 Tbsp of lime juice and toss to coat.
Combine the yogurt, honey, ginger, salt, and final Tbsp of lime juice in a small bowl. Add to the mango mixture. Add mint and toss to combine. Before serving, place in the fridge for at least 15 minutes.

Nutrition Facts (1 portion):

Energy: 105 Kcal
Carbs: 26g
Proteins: 1g
Fats: 1g

Fats: 23 g

11. Tangy Curry Pasta Salad

Portion Size: 2
Duration: 30 minutes

Ingredients:

½ bag pasta shells
1 sweet onion
1 green pepper
½ cup ketchup
¼ cup oil
tabasco sauce
½ cup sugar
1 tbsp curry powder
¼ cup vinegar
Ground pepper
garnish: Parsley

Instructions:

Cook pasta in salted water until done then drain.
Add the finely chopped green pepper and onion to the cooked pasta.
Incorporate all of the other components in order to create the sauce, then thoroughly combine with the pasta.
The leftovers, if any, taste much better the next day after the pasta has absorbed some of the sauce, so refrigerate.
Add parsley as a garnish.

Nutrition Facts (1 portion):

Energy: 501 Kcal
Carbs: 73 g
Proteins: 4 g

12. Vegetable Salad Recipe

Portion Size: 2
Duration: 20 min

Ingredients:

1/4 small package. lemon jelly
3/8 cups boiling water
1/8 of a cup of salad dressing
1/2 carrot -peeled and shredded
1/4 of celery, chopped
1/2 tsp. onion, diced
1/4 of a small green pepper, diced fine
1/4 of a small carton of cottage cheese
1/4 of a small container of whip, cooled

Instructions:

Combine the boiling water with the jelly.
Shake until dissolved.
Let stand until just starting to set up.
Carrots, celery, onion, green pepper, and salad dressing are added.
Mix slowly.
Cottage cheese and Cool Whip should be folded in.
Chill.

Nutrition Facts (1 portion):

Energy: 247 Kcal
Carbs: 11g
Proteins: 5g
Fats: 20g

13. Buko Salad Recipe

Portion Size: 2
Duration: 130 min

Ingredients:

1/5-quart heavy cream
1/5 (14 oz) can condensed milk
3/5 (30 oz) cans fruit cocktail, drained
2/5 (14 oz) packages coconut
1/5 liter of kaong, palm nut

Instructions:

Mix each component together. Place for two hours in the freezer.

Nutrition Facts (1 portion):

Energy: 387 Kcal
Carbs: 8 g
Proteins: 2.3 g
Fats: 39 g

14. Mango-Peach Smoothie

Portion Size: 2
Duration: 5 min

Ingredients:

1/2 a cup of milk, fat-free
1/2 a cup of yogurt, peach flavor
1 cup of mango chunks, frozen

Instructions:

Blend all items in a covered container until smooth. Serve right away.

Nutrition Facts (1 portion):

Energy: 180 Kcal
Carbs: 39g
Proteins: 6g
Fats: 1g

15. Mushroom & Zucchini Pesto Saute

Portion Size: 2
Duration: 10 minutes

Ingredients:

1 tsp olive oil
1/4 of a lb. of fresh mushrooms, sliced
1/2 small onion, chopped
1 medium sized zucchini, sliced
1 1/2 Tbsps. prepared pesto
1/8 tsp of pepper and lemon seasoning

Instructions:

Heat oil in a large pan.
Put onion as well as mushrooms in it, then heat and stir for two minutes. Add, Cook and stir the zucchini until it is soft. Add the lemon-pepper spice and pesto.

Nutrition Facts (1 portion):

Energy: 99 Kcal
Carbs: 8 g
Proteins: 4 g
Fats: 7 g

16. Hearty Asian Lettuce Salad

Portion Size: 2
Duration: 20 min

Ingredients:

1 cup ready-to-eat brown rice
1 cup of shelled edamame, frozen
3 cups spring mix lettuce greens
1/4 cup sesame ginger salad dressing (reduced fat)
1medium-sized orange
4 radishes, sliced
2 tbsp of browned, chopped almonds

Instructions:

Follow the guidelines on the box to prepare the rice and edamame.
Combine salad greens, rice, and edamame inside a big container. Incorporate dressing and mix.
Divide the salad across two plates and garnish with the almonds, radishes, and orange segments.

Nutrition Facts (1 portion):

Energy: 329 Kcal
Carbs: 44 g
Proteins: 13 g
Fats: 10 g

17. Apple-White Cheddar Grilled Cheese

Portion Size: 2
Duration: 20 minutes

Ingredients:

3 oz of cheddar cheese
1 thin slice red onion, separated into rings
4 slices whole wheat cinnamon-raisin bread
1/4 of a tsp of pepper flakes
1 small size apple, thinly sliced
1 Tbsp butter, softened

Instructions:

Cheese is placed one slice between each pair of bread slices. Add apple and onion on top.
Add a couple of pepper flakes, if favored.
Add the remaining bread and cheese over top. Butter should be spread on the outsides of the sandwiches' outsides. Toast sandwiches for three to five mins until golden in color.

Nutrition Facts (1 portion):

Energy: 456Kcal
Carbs: 37 g
Proteins: 20 g
Fats: 27 g

18. Zucchini Pancakes

Portion Size: 2
Duration: 20 minutes

Ingredients:

1 1/2 cups of grated zucchini
3 tbsp of finely grated Parmesan cheese
1 big egg, lightly beaten with a dash of pepper
1 Tbsp canola oil
2 Tbsps. biscuit/baking mix
Sour cream, optional

Instructions:

Drain the zucchini. Use paper towels to dry after you squeeze. Take a container and combine the pepper, cheese, baking mix, and egg. Put zucchini in it and mix. Heat oil in a big skillet at medium heat. Four pancakes should be dropped into the griddle and gently flattened. Cook on each side for about two mins. Have with sour cream, if preferred.

Nutrition Facts (1 portion):

Energy: 174 Kcal
Carbs: 9g
Proteins: 7g
Fats: 13g

19. Grilled Mixed Fruit & Vegetable Kabobs

Portion Size: 2
Duration: 20 minutes

Ingredients:
1/2 organic bell pepper, diced
6 fresh pineapple chunks
1/2 organic zucchini, cut
1 Tbsp Basting Oil
1/2 sweet onion, quartered
1/2 Tbsp Balsamic Vinegar
Pepper and salt as desired

Instructions:

Warm up the grill. In a mixing dish, combine balsamic vinegar and basting oil. Thread three pieces of each veggie and pineapple onto skewers in whichever order you like. Brush the skewers with 1 tablespoon oil and vinegar. Grill for about 10 minutes, flipping every three minutes, or until the grill marks appear and the vegetables crisp. Pour the remaining vinegar and oil mixture on top. Season with pepper and salt to taste. Remove the skewers and serve in the dish.

Nutrition Facts (1 portion):

Energy: 120 Kcal
Carbs: 17 g
Proteins: 2 g
Fats: 6 g

20. Fruit Crisp

Portion Size: 2
Duration: 25 minutes

Ingredients:

1/4 of a cup of brown sugar
1 cup fruit, peeled and sliced
1/6 cup flour
3 tbsp instant oats
a dash of ginger powder
1/3 of tsp Ceylon cinnamon

Instructions:

Turn on the 375-degree oven.
In an 8x8-inch baking dish, arrange the fruit.
Thoroughly mixing the remaining Ingredient and sprinkle over the fruit
Bake until golden brown (30 min).
Prior to serving, allow standing for 30 minutes.

Nutrition Facts (1 portion):
Energy: 703Kcal
Carbs: 110g
Proteins: 7 g
Fats: 29 g

Fish and Seafood

1. Fish Dreams Recipe

Portion Size: 2
Duration: 45 min

Ingredients:

1 lb. fish
1 egg
1/8 tsp of paprika
1 Tbsp of flour
a pinch of salt

Instructions:

Fish filets should be simmered in a tiny amount of water for around 5 minutes so they flake easily. Let come to room temperature and drain.
Divide up the egg whites and yolks.
Beat the egg yolks, add salt, flour, and paprika. Add the fish and stir well. Beat egg whites until peaks appear. Fold in fish mixture.
Fry in hot grease till golden brown before flipping over to finish cooking the other side.

Nutrition Facts (1 portion):
Energy: 719Kcal
Carbs: 25g
Proteins: 55g
Fats: 44g

2. Fish Stock Recipe

Portion Size: 2
Duration: 21 min

Ingredients:

8 4/5 oz fish, lugs and bits (any leftover bits will do, including heads)
a pinch of salt
1/4 of tsp of cracked pepper
1 tsp lemon (no skin)
1/2 bay leaves
1/6 large onion, brown, unpeeled and chopped
1/2 medium carrots, chopped roughly
1/10 cup white wine

Instructions:

Place the fish in a stockpot, cover with water, and bring to a boil.
Wait around 40 minutes after turning off the heat.
You can now take any valuable flesh and put it in the fridge.
Bring the stock back up to a simmer.
Simmer for 30 minutes, depending on the thickness of your lugs.
The stock should not be cooked because it will get bitter. If the consistency needs to be reduced, drain it first and then boil it until the desired consistency is attained.

Nutrition Facts (1 portion):

Energy: 383Kcal
Carbs: 15g
Proteins: 29 g
Fats: 22 g

3. Sea Scallops Sauteed with Mushrooms & Pasta

Portion Size: 2
Duration: 20 min
Ingredients:

2/3 lb. sea scallops, quartered (about 10 large)
5 1/3 oz pasta (about 3 cups cooked al dente)
2 oz fresh mushrooms (about 8 medium sliced)
2 tbsp butter
2 Garlic cloves
1/4 cup white wine
2/3 tsp freshly ground sea salt
2 Tbsps. of lemon juice, fresh

Instructions:

Scallops should be washed and drained.
Melt 2 tablespoons butter in a saucepan. Add scallops and one smashed garlic clove.
Cook over medium heat, stirring regularly.
Scallops should be taken from the pan, leaving the liquid behind. Pour in the wine, two tablespoons lemon juice, two crushed garlic cloves, and the mushrooms. Sauté for around 3 minutes. Melt the butter and add the noodles. Stir in the cooked scallops, 1 teaspoon sea salt, and the lemon juice. Stir, cover, remove from heat, and let aside for 5 minutes before mixing, and it's ready to serve.

Nutrition Facts (1 portion):

Energy: 408Kcal
Carbs: 30g
Proteins: 37g
Fats: 13g

4. Grilled Shrimp in the Shell

Portion Size: 2
Duration: 15 min
Ingredients:

1 lb. Fresh Wild Caught Shrimp, 1 lb.
Pepper and salt to your liking
3 Tbsps. of olive oil

Instructions:

Set the grill to HIGH.
Add shrimp in a big container and put in salt with pepper.
Pour oil over and coat by tossing.
Grill the shrimp and then cover.
2 to 3 minutes of grilling.
Flip over.
2 to 3 minutes of grilling.
Take the grill off (130 degrees).
Rest for 2 minutes (at 145 degrees).
Serve with cocktail sauce if desired for more flavor.

Nutrition Facts (1 portion):

Energy: 190 Kcal
Carbs: 0g
Proteins: 36g
Fats: 5g

5. Grilled Scallop Kabob

Portion Size: 2
Duration: 30 min

Ingredients:
1/4 yellow bell pepper, diced
1/4 Green Bell Pepper, diced
1/4 orange bell pepper, diced
1/4 red onion, layered
10 Sea Scallops, Fresh

Instructions:

For 10 minutes, preheat the grill to HIGH.
To make kabobs, alternate peppers, onions, and scallops on sticks.
Using a delicate cloth, apply a thin layer of vegetable oil on the grill grate.
Brush the kabobs with a thin layer of basting oil.
Lower the heat after grilling the kabobs for a few minutes on each side.
Cook for 10-12 minutes, or until the scallops reach an internal temperature of 130°.
Midway through, insert a thermometer into the thickest part of the scallop.
Place it on a clean platter and rest it for at least two minutes.

Nutrition Facts (1 portion):

Energy: 200Kcal
Carbs: 22g
Proteins: 16g
Fats: 6g

6. Grilled Oysters

Portion Size: 2
Duration: 20 min

Ingredients:

6 living oysters

Instructions:

Turn the grill on HIGH for 10 minutes. Cleanly rinse oysters in cold, running water.
Place oysters directly on the grill, flat side up, and cover. Open oysters after 6 to 8 minutes of cooking.
With tongs, remove the oysters from the grill. After carefully dragging a knife along the shell edge to open, throw away the top shell.
Serve right away.

Nutrition Facts (1 portion):

Energy: 25Kcal
Carbs: 1g
Proteins: 3g
Fats: 1g

7. Soft Shell Crab Sandwich

Portion Size: 2
Duration: 25 minutes
Ingredients:

2 Ready to Cook Prime Soft Shell Crabs Tempura, cooked per pkg Instructions
2 Brioche Rolls, sliced, toasted
2 Tbsp Remoulade Sauce divided
2 leaves Green Butter Lettuce, divided
2 slices Organic Tomatoes on the Vine, divided

Instructions:

Each roll's bottom is uniformly spread with 1 Tbsp sauce; cooked crab, 1 lettuce leaf, and 1 tomato slice are then placed on top of each roll.

Nutrition Facts (1 portion):

Energy: 530Kcal
Carbs: 60g
Proteins: 18g
Fats: 25g

8. Sea Scallops Brochette with Pernod Sauce

Portion Size: 2
Duration: 20 minutes
Ingredients:

8 sea scallops
2 tbsp Pernod
4 tbsp light sour cream
2 stalks fresh rosemary
1/2 Tbsp of olive oil
Pepper and salt, as desired

Instructions:

Rinse the scallops carefully to eliminate debris. Scallops should be strained before drying with a soft paper towel.
After cleaning the rosemary stems properly, carefully connect four scallops to each stem.
Cook each side of the brochettes for 2 minutes in a nonstick pan with olive oil.
Set them aside on a platter and season with pepper and salt. (Keep the food warm.).
Pour Pernod into the pan and light it on fire. Season with a small amount of mild sour cream.
Pernod sauce should be paired with sea scallops.

Nutrition Facts (1 portion):
Energy: 64Kcal
Carbs: 1.8 g
Proteins: 1g
Fats: 6g

9. Fish Bake

Portion Size: 2
Duration: 18 min
Ingredients:

1/2-pound fish filet
1/2 egg
1/2 cup of coarse breadcrumbs
1 Tbsp of milk
1/8 of a tsp of salt
1/4 tsp Dry mustard
1/8 tsp of fresh ground pepper
1 Tbsp of olive oil
1/4 of tsp Italian herb seasoning

Instructions:
Set the oven to 450 degrees.
Cut thick fish filets into the appropriate sizes.
Combine egg and milk. Mix the crumbs, salt, dry mustard, Italian herb spice, and pepper in another container.
Dip fish in egg mixture, followed by the bread crumbs; firmly press the fish into the crumbs
On a baking pan with hot oil, place the fillets. To make sure all sides are greased, flip over right away.
Bake for 4 min on each side.

Nutrition Facts (1 portion):
Energy: 467Kcal
Carbs: 21g
Proteins: 29g
Fats: 29g

10. Seafood Omelet

Portion Size: 2
Duration: 2 min

Ingredients:
1/2 of crab, imitation works
2 green onions
1 tsp cheese
4 or 3 eggs
butter
pepper and salt, as desired

Instructions:

Crab is chopped, along with onions and capers. Place aside. Smash eggs.
Butter will melt in a pan.
Add the egg, then add the crab, onions, and capers on top.
Sprinkle cheese when almost done, then place the plate halfway on it and flip.
Pepper and salt as desired.

Nutrition Facts (1 portion):
Energy: 185Kcal
Carbs: 11g
Proteins: 16g
Fats: 22 g

11. Szechuan Shrimp with Mushrooms & Peppers

Portion Size: 2
Duration: 15 min

Ingredients:
1 Tbsp Soy Sauce
1 pkg (5 oz) Organic Sliced Shiitake Mushrooms, washed
1/4 cup Szechuan Sauce
1/2 Red Bell Pepper, diced
1 Tbsp of Olive Oil
1 pkg (1 lb.) Organic Large Raw Shrimp, thawed per pkg Instructions
4 green onions, trimmed, sliced
Pepper and salt
1/2 Tbsp Garlic Cheese Finishing Butter
Juice of 1/2 lime (about 1 Tbsp)

Instructions:
Mix Szechuan sauce and soy sauce and whisk it. Oil should be heated on MED-HIGH until oil just begins to smoke. Toss in and cook the red pepper and mushroom for three minutes.
Add the prawns, pepper and salt.
2 min of cooking while stirring.
Add the green onions, butter, and sauce mixture. About 1 minute, while stirring, or until thoroughly heated. Place on a serving platter and top with lime juice.

Nutrition Facts (1 portion):
Energy: 340 Kcal
Carbs: 13g
Proteins: 33g
Fats: 17g

12. Pan-Seared Salmon with Mustard Sauce

Portion Size: 2
Duration: 20 min

Ingredients:

2 (6 oz each) Fresh Skinless Atlantic Salmon Portions
Pepper and salt
1/2 Tbsp of Olive Oil
1/4 cup of Mustard Sauce
1/2Tbsp of Basting Oil
Pan Searing Flour
1/2 tsp Organic Salted Butter

Instructions:
Season the fish with pepper and salt.
Optional: Lightly flour both sides for pan searing and shake off excess.
After the olive oil has heated, add the fish to the pan. Cook for 3 minutes, or until the color changes halfway up and the seared side is browned.
Turn it over. When the internal temperature of the fish reaches 120 degrees, it has been cooked for around 3 minutes.
In the skillet, swirl in the butter and basting oil. Spoon the batter until it reaches 130 degrees (1-3 minutes).
Place the fish on a clean dish and let aside for at least two minutes.
Serve with Mustard Sauce.

Nutrition Facts (1 portion):
Energy: 550 Kcal
Carbs: 1 g
Proteins: 36 g
Fats: 40 g

13. Horseradish Crusted Salmon

Portion Size: 2
Duration: 25 min
Ingredients:

Organic Olive Oil Cooking Spray
2 (6 oz each) Fresh Skinless Atlantic Salmon Portions
Pepper and salt
1/8 of a cup of Basting Oil
1 Tbsp Prepared Horseradish
1/2 cup White Panko Bread Crumbs
2 tsp Horseradish Mustard, divided

Instructions:

Preheat the oven to 450°F.
Spray the baking sheet with cooking spray.
Season the fish with pepper and salt before placing it in the pan.
In a separate container, combine the panko and horseradish with the basting oil.
1 tsp horseradish mustard on top of each portion of salmon, followed by 1/4 of the horseradish-panko mixture.
Bake for 14 minutes, or until the salmon reaches 130°F (test by inserting a thermometer halfway into the thickest part of the fish). Wait two minutes after turning off the oven.

Nutrition Facts (1 portion):
Energy: 490 Kcal
Carbs: 12g
Proteins: 37g
Fats: 30g

14. Salmon with Pesto

Portion Size: 2
Duration: 20 min
Ingredients:

2 (6 oz each) Fresh Skinless Atlantic Salmon Portions
4 Tbsp Italian Classics Basil Pesto Sauce, divided
4 Tbsp Italian Classics Shredded Parmigiano Reggiano, divided
2 Tbsp White Panko Bread Crumbs, divided
1/2 Tbsp Basting Oil

Instructions:

Make sure the oven is at 350 degrees.
Spread 2 Tbsp pesto over each salmon chunk, followed by 2 Tbsp cheese and 1 Tbsp panko.
Apply basting oil sparingly to the baking pan's bottom.
Salmon should be placed side up in a pan.
When the internal temperature of the salmon reaches 145 degrees, it has been baked for 18 to 20 mins.

Nutrition Facts (1 portion):
Energy: 600 Kcal
Carbs: 5g
Proteins: 43g
Fats: 42g

15. Sea Bass with Citrus-Olive-Caper Sauce

Portion Size: 2
Duration: 20 min
Ingredients:

1 skinned sea bass filet
1/8 of a tsp of black pepper
1/3 of a cup Olive oil, a third of a cup
1/2 Tbsp. rinsed capers
1/4 tsp salt
1/2 lemon, sliced
lemon juice
1 Tbsp, Fresh oregano, chopped
1/5 cup chopped olives

Instructions:

The grill should be placed close to the heating element.
On a dish, brush the filets with 1 tablespoon of oil on both sides. The pan should be carefully removed from the oven and placed on the fire. Place the filets in a skillet (skin side down) and season with pepper and salt.
 Salmon broiling for 6 minutes. In a mixing dish, combine the lemon slices, juice, oregano, capers, olives, remaining salt, oil, and pepper. Place the fish on a plate and drizzle with the citrus-olive-caper sauce.

Nutrition Facts (1 portion):

Energy: 231Kcal
Carbs: 5g
Proteins: 26g
Fats: 11g

Burgers

1. Double cheeseburger

Portion Size: 2
Duration: 25 min

Ingredients:
400 g of beef mince
3 tsps. Worcestershire sauce
3 tsp Tomato Puree
2 tsps. Mustard Powder
1 smashed garlic clove
2 tsps. olive oil
2 cheddar cheese slices
2 hamburger buns, halves
Salt & black pepper add to taste
Mayonnaise and tomato ketchup

Instructions:
In a mixing dish, combine the beef mince, tomato puree, Worcestershire sauce, salt, and mustard powder.
Divide the mixture into four equal parts and flatten into patties.
Warm the olive oil in a nonstick frying pan.
Burger patties should be brushed with olive oil and grilled for two minutes on each side, until lightly browned.
Remove it and place it on one of the hamburger buns.
Place another patty on top of the cheese slice.
Top the patty with lettuce and tomato slices.
After spreading mayonnaise on it, place the second half of the bun on top.
With tomato ketchup, serve.

Nutrition Facts (1 portion):

Energy: 655 Kcal
Carbs: 35g
Proteins: 40g
Fats: 45g

2. Mediterranean turkey burger

Portion Size: 2
Duration: 25 min

Ingredients:
2 frozen turkey burgers
1 full roasted red pepper
2 English muffins or four whole grain buns
tapenade of Kalamata olives
1/4 cup cottage cheese
1 sun-dried tomato in oil
1/2 clove of garlic, chopped
1/8 cup chopped cilantro with tabasco and jalapeno sauce
Salt & pepper

Instructions:

Make the cheese sauce by mixing all of the ingredients with the cheese.
Using a blender, make a thick paste.
You may need to add a little milk or yogurt to achieve the desired consistency.
Season with salt and pepper to taste.
Burgers can be grilled or fried in a skillet.
For the last minute of cooking, add half of a roasted red pepper on the top to heat through. Buns can be baked or toasted.
Tapenade is put on the bottom side of the bun.
On top, place a heated burger with pepper.
Top with the remaining muffin or bun half and a generous schmear of cheese sauce.

Nutrition Facts (1 portion):

Energy: 172 Kcal
Carbs: 30g
Proteins: 8.2g
Fats: 2.4g

3. Zinger burger

Portion Size: 2
Duration: 50 min

Ingredients:

1 Chicken breast
2 hamburger buns
mayonnaise
salad leaves
oil to fry
Chicken margination
1/4 tsp. salt and white pepper
1/2 tsp. black pepper
1 egg
1/2 tsp of red chili powder, crushed
to Coat
4 Tbsps. each of plain flour, corn flour and baking powder ½ tsp
For seasoning, use salt & black pepper

Instructions:

After slicing the chicken breast horizontally into two narrower sections, flatten it with a hammer.
In a jar, combine the marinade ingredients. Allow to sit for two hours on the chicken breast.
On a dish, chicken slices are coated with a mixture of the coating's ingredients.
Place these pieces on another dish, briefly damp both sides, and then dust with flour again.
Fry in oil over a medium heat.
Apply mayonnaise to both halves of a hamburger bun, then toast till golden in a pan. Place a lettuce leaf, chicken, and mayonnaise on one bun and top with another.
Serve immediately.

Nutrition Facts (1 portion):
Energy: 380 Kcal
Carbs: 18g
Proteins: 27g
Fats: 6g

4. Spicy Mexican bean burger

Portion Size: 2
Duration: 15min

Ingredients:

1/2 can of vegan refried fat-free beans
Oil, half a tsp
finely minced small onions, 1/4 of a cup
1/4 green pepper coarsely diced
2 burger buns
1/2 of a peeled and shredded carrot
Hot & picante sauce
1/2 a cup of breadcrumbs
1/4 cup of flour
salt, as desired
1/2 tsp black pepper
1/2 a dash of Cumin and pepper flakes
1/4 cup of sliced black olives

Instructions:

In a skillet over medium heat, heat the oil. Combine the carrots, corn, onions, and green peppers in a mixing bowl.
Meanwhile, combine the beans in a large mixing dish.
Cook until the vegetables are brilliantly colored. After adding the vegetables, blend the beans with a hand mixer. Add the other ingredients, adjusting the consistency with more flour if the mixture is too fragile or more salsa if it is too thick. Make balls, then flatten them into patties. Place on wax paper and stack in Tupperware. Place five or more sliced olives in the center of the patty. To envelop, squash.
Spray each burger with frying oil before heating. Cook over medium heat until one side is browned. If desired, flip the burger over and drizzle with hot sauce. Serve them with salsa, chopped onion, and a slice of cheese on a toasted hamburger bun.

Nutrition Facts (1 portion):
Energy: 313Kcal
Carbs: 42 g
Proteins: 7g

Fats: 12.9g

5. Bistro Burger

Portion Size: 2
Duration: 35 min

Ingredients:
2 hamburger buns
4 slices cheddar cheese
½ lb. ground sirloin
Salt & black pepper
1 tbsp. mayonnaise
½ tbsp. Dijon mustard
½ tbsp. olive oil & butter
¼ tsp brown sugar
Ruffles potato chip
1 large sweet onion

Instructions:
Sauce: In a jar, combine the sauce's ingredients. Set aside to allow the flavors to combine. To make VIDALIA, melt the butter and oil in a sauté pan over low heat. Add the diced onion and brown sugar, then boil the stew for 20 to 30 minutes, stirring frequently, until the onion has caramelized. Set them aside while they are still heated. Make the burgers: While you're making the burgers, preheat the grill or a cast iron pan to high. Using ground sirloin, make four burgers. Season both sides with salt and pepper to taste. Grill or pan-fry for three to four minutes on each side for medium-rare doneness. In the final minutes of cooking, add two pieces of cheese to each burger, followed by caramelized onions. Cover the grill or pan for approximately a minute to allow the cheese to melt. Before assembling, spread Bistro sauce on the bottoms of the toasted buns. Attach the hamburgers to the buns. Top with the indicated toppings.

Nutrition Facts (1 portion):
Energy: 689Kcal
Carbs: 45g

Proteins: 43g
Fats: 36g

6. Cherry and Brie Burger

Portion Size: 2
Duration: 60 min

Ingredients:
4 Tbsps. bulgur wheat or fine grain
2 cups of onion, roughly sliced
2 large garlic cloves
4 tbsp of olive oil
1/2 cup of mayonnaise
1 1/2 tsp. pepper, divided, and 5 tsps. freshly cut rosemary
2 cups of tart dried cherries
2 tbsp. kosher salt
2 lbs. of bison or lean ground beef
8 oz Brie cheese cut into slices for burgers
8 hamburger buns with sesame butter, divided
lettuce

Instructions:
Combine bulgur and 1/3 cup boiling water in a 2-cup glass measuring cup. Wait 10 minutes before reheating for 2 to 3 minutes in the microwave, or until the liquid is absorbed. Turn down the heat. Meanwhile, in a large frying pan over medium heat, sauté chopped onion in 1 tablespoon oil for 10 to 15 minutes, flipping periodically, until deep golden. The garlic is then scraped into a large dish to cool. Brush the onion slices with the remaining 1 tablespoon oil and set aside. In a mixing dish, combine mayonnaise, 1/4 teaspoon pepper, and 1/2 teaspoon rosemary. Chill. Heat the grill to medium (350 to 450 degrees). Cherries should be powdered up and rolled into balls in a food processor. Add the remaining 2 teaspoons rosemary, 12 teaspoon pepper, salt, and bulgur to the chopped onion and mix thoroughly with your hands. After adding the ground meat, gently but completely mix it in. Make 4 1/2-inch-thick patties. Grill the onion slices for 10 to 15 minutes, flipping once or twice, until beautifully browned. Grill the burgers for 10 to 12 minutes total, flipping once

with a broad spatula, or until they no longer adhere to the grill and grill marks form. Top the burgers with brie and broil the buns for 2 minutes before they're done.

After putting mayonnaise on the buns, top with lettuce, hamburgers, and onions.

Nutrition Facts (1 portion):
Energy: 1900Kcal
Carbs: 41g
Proteins: 124g
Fats: 137g

Reapply frying spray to the same skillet and cook the patties in butter for three to five minutes on each side, or until slightly charred. Serve with cheese, lettuce, and tomato on buns.

Nutrition Facts (1 portion):
Energy: 433Kcal
Carbs: 74g
Proteins: 18g
Fats: 6g

7. Veggie Tuna Burger

Portion Size: 2
Duration: 30 min

Ingredients:
1/10 cup of coarsely sliced onion
1/3 garlic clove, minced
1/3 each of shredded carrots, zucchini, and yellow summer squash
Lightly beat 1/3 of an egg
2/3 cups soft whole wheat bread crumbs
1/3 can (6 oz.) drained and shredded light water-packed tuna
pepper, salt; as desired
1/4 tsp of butter
Splitting 2 hamburger buns
2 slices of cheddar cheese with less fat
2 pieces of lettuce, 2 slices of tomato

Instructions:
In a large nonstick skillet sprayed with cooking spray, sauté the onion and garlic for one minute. Cook the carrots, zucchini, and yellow squash until they are soft. Allow to cool to room temperature after draining.

In a large mixing bowl, combine the egg, bread crumbs, tuna, salt, and pepper. The vegetable mixture is now added. Divide the mixture into two 3-1/2-inch patties.

8. Chicken burger

Portion Size: 2
Duration: 40 min

Ingredients:

2/3 lb. of minced chicken
1/6 cup of ketchup
2/3 tbsp. of mustard
salt, pepper, and a clove of minced garlic with one-third of an onion

Instructions:

Stir the onion and garlic together until they are soft and starting to brown.
Together, properly combine all the ingredients.
Separate into two equal parts.
Form into burger patties.
Spray oil on a frying pan and then fry the burgers, flipping once, until fully done.

Nutrition Facts (1 portion):

Energy: 334Kcal
Carbs: 14 g
Proteins: 27g
Fats: 19g

9. Smash Burger

Portion Size: 2
Duration: 25 min

Ingredients:

½ tbsp. sunflower oil
2 burger buns sesame topped
250g steak minced
2 slices cheddar cheese
1 red onion finely chopped
1 sliced tomato
Mayonnaise
ketchup
A handful of iceberg lettuce shredded finely

Instructions:

Cut the hamburger buns in half, toast or broil the cut sides, and set aside. The oven temperature has been set at 200° gas. Season the mince with salt and pepper to taste, then divide it into two heaps. One of the stacks is placed in a heavy skillet or frying pan that has been heated over high heat with 1/4 tbsp oil. Working fast, cover the beef patty with a square of parchment paper and press it into a smaller pan as solid as possible (you can use the end of a rolling pin or oven gloves for this, but be careful of the heat and rising steam). Allow it to cook for 2 minutes. After removing the parchment, flip the burger over. Cook for one minute, then use a spatula to press down and top with a slice of cheese. Transfer the remaining burgers to a baking sheet and keep them warm in the oven while you cook the remaining burgers in the same manner. Before adding a smashed patty, gherkin slices, and the top bun, arrange slices of onion, lettuce, and tomato on a bun foundation. Serves with your choice of sauces on the side.

Nutrition Facts (1 portion):
Energy: 666Kcal

Carbs: 41g
Proteins: 37g
Fats: 39g

Fats: 20g

10. Chicken Caesar burger

Portion Size: 2
Duration: 30 min

Ingredients:
1/4 of a cup of finely chopped onion
2 Tbsps. Split parmesan cheese
1Tbsp Lemon juice,
1 1/2 Tbsps. of fresh parsley flakes
1 minced clove of garlic
1 Tbsp Worcestershire sauce
1/4 of a tsp of salt
1/8 of a tsp of Pepper
1/2 a lb. of chicken meat
2 split hamburger buns
Romaine lettuce, shredded into 1/4 cup
4 Tbsps. Caesar salad dressing

Instructions:

In a separate bowl, mix the onion, 1 Tbsp of the cheese, parsley, garlic, lemon juice, Worcestershire sauce, salt, and pepper. Stir thoroughly before adding the crumbled chicken. The ingredients will yield two patties.
When a meat thermometer reads 165 degrees and the juices run clear, burgers should be covered and cooked for 5-7 minutes on each side. Top with the remaining cheese.
Salad dressing and romaine lettuce are served on buns.

Nutrition Facts (1 portion):

Energy: 467Kcal
Carbs: 40g
Proteins: 30g

11. Spinach Feta Burger

Portion Size: 2
Duration: 20 min

Ingredients:
1 cup of fresh spinach, torn
1/8 cup feta cheese crumbles
1/8 cup finely sliced plum tomatoes
1/2 green onions, chopped
1/4 tsp dill
1/4 tsp of pepper and salt
1/2 lbs. of ground beef
2 split hamburger buns

Instructions:

In a big basin, mix the first seven Ingredients. Stir thoroughly after adding the crumbled meat to the stew. Into two 4-inch patties, shape.
When the meat temperature is 160°, grill for four-five mins each side / broil 4 inches from the flame. serving with buns.

Nutrition Facts (1 portion):

Energy: 446 Kcal
Carbs: 37 g
Proteins: 30 g
Fats: 20 g

12. Chicken Cheese Burger

Portion Size: 2
Duration: 20 min

Ingredients:

2 burger buns
2 slices cheddar cheese
1/8 cup ranch dressing
1 halved chicken breast
1/8 cup salsa sauce
2 lettuces loose leaf

Instructions:

Take a pan and add oil to it before beginning to create these scrumptious hamburgers. It is heated to medium heat. Add the chicken after the oil is heated enough, and cook for between five and seven minutes. Remove the chicken from the fire after it has finished cooking, then place it on a plate.
Now, using a knife, cut the hamburger buns in half. In the meantime, cover the bottom half with ranch dressing. After placing a lettuce leaf on it, the cooked chicken should be placed there. Top with salsa, and cheese and cover with the other half of the bun. Allow it to lay for 2 minutes.
serve with your choice of a chilled beverage.

Nutrition Facts (1 portion):

Energy: 446 Kcal
Carbs: 32g
Proteins: 27g
Fats: 14g

13. Tandoori chicken burger

Portion Size: 2
Duration: 45 min

Ingredients:

2 Chicken Breast Fillets, Skinless and Boneless
1 tbsp. of Tandoori Masala Powder
1/4 cup plain yogurt
3 tsps. finely chopped mint leaves
2 burger buns, cut in half
1 small, thinly sliced tomato
1 onion and cucumbers diced
1 small or finely cut carrot
1 cup chopped mixed salad leaves, a few torn lettuce leaves
Oil, 1/2 to 1 tbsp.

Instructions:

To the tandoori masala powder, add 2 tablespoons plain water. In a mixing bowl, combine the paste and two tablespoons of yoghurt. Stir in the chicken pieces until they are equally covered. Set aside for 5 to 10 minutes. Warm the oil in a nonstick skillet over medium heat. After five to ten minutes of marinating, the chicken should be well cooked and browned. Combine the yogurt and 1/4 cup mint leaves in a mixing bowl. Lightly toast the buns before placing them on a flat surface, if preferred. Spread the yogurt and mint mixture on the halves. Garnish with lettuce, salad leaves, cucumber, carrots, and onions. Then top with the remaining half of the cooked chicken patty.
Serve immediately with fries or a salad.

Nutrition Facts (1 portion):
Energy: 465 Kcal
Carbs: 35g

Proteins: 25g
Fats: 28g

14. Chicken Cordons Bleu burger

Portion Size: 2
Duration: 30 min

Ingredients:

2 Tbsp sour cream
1 Tbsp powdered yellow mustard
1/10 cups honey
1 flattened, boneless, skinless chicken breast half
1/3 tsp of onion powder
Swiss cheese, and deli ham on two pieces each.
2 onions buns

Instructions:

Preheat the oven's grill while placing the baking rack about six inches above the heat source. In a small mixing dish, combine the honey, mustard, and sour cream. Place in the refrigerator until ready to use.
Divide each chicken breast into two equal halves. Sprinkle onion powder on both sides of the chicken breasts. In a large skillet, heat the nonstick frying spray over medium-high heat. In the oven, brown the bottoms of the chicken breasts. Top the chicken with a slice of cheddar and some gammon after flipping it. The chicken should be fully cooked and the cheese melted.
Place the buns on the grill, cut side up. Toast until a faint browning emerges on the surface.

Serve each chicken cordon bleu burger with a tsp of honey-mustard sauce on toasted onion buns.

Nutrition Facts (1 portion):
Energy: 673Kcal
Carbs: 50g
Proteins: 66 g
Fats: 25g

15. Turkey burger with special sauce

Portion Size: 2
Duration: 25 min

Ingredients:

1/8 cup finely minced onions (green)
1tbsp orange juice, fresh
1/2 tbsp soy sauce low sodium
1/2 tsp coarsely chopped fresh ginger, peeled
1/2 a minced garlic clove
cooking spray for half a pound of ground turkey breast
1/8 cup of special sauce
2 whole wheat hamburger buns
a pair of wavy lettuce leaf

Instructions:

Preheat the grill.
Combine the initial six Ingredients in a container. Make 2 equally sized portions of the turkey mixture, and then form patty. Put the patties on a grill, and bake for six mins on both sides till they're cooked. On the top of each bun, spoon 2 Tbsps. of Special Sauce. Lay lettuce leaves, and patty between burger buns. Slice each hamburger in half.

Nutrition Facts (1 portion):

Energy: 301Kcal
Carbs: 18g
Proteins: 27g
Fats: 7g

16. Vegan black bean burger

Portion Size: 2
Duration: 65 min

Ingredients:

1/4 tsp egg substitute
1/4 tbsp. water and egg replacer combined
1/8 tsp. cumin, onion, and garlic powder
1/8 of a can of refried beans
1/10 tsp of chipotle powder
1 1/2 cup chopped mushrooms
1/8 whole onion, big diced, sautéed
1/5 cup whole wheat breadcrumbs
1/8 can rinsed and drained black beans

Instructions:

Preheat the oven to 350 F.
Combine the ingredients in a blender. Put in a large, empty dish. Add the 'Other' Ingredients one at a time, bending them in completely before adding the next. A pasty mixture should form.
Preheat the oven to 350°F. Line two cookie sheets with parchment paper. By adding 1/2 cup of the ingredients, pressing down, and raising the cutter, you may create a perfectly round disc-shaped patty.

Repeat to make two patties. After placing in the oven, bake for 15 minutes. After you've turned them all over, return them to the oven for another 10 minutes. Take out and top with your favorite burger buns and toppings.

Nutrition Facts (1 portion):
Energy: 80Kcal
Carbs: 13g
Proteins: 5g
Fats: 1.3g

17. Steakhouse Burger

Portion Size: 2
Duration: 25 min

Ingredients:

2 sandwich bread pieces
1/3 cup of milk
1/2 tsp kosher salt
1/2 tsp black pepper
1 garlic clove, minced
1/2 tbsp Worcestershire sauce
2 tsps. Ketchup
1 pound of lean beef
2 hamburger buns

Instructions:

Preheat the grill to high heat.
To make a thick mixture, thoroughly combine the milk and bread in a large mixing basin. After adding the Worcestershire sauce, ketchup, salt, pepper, and garlic, combine well.
After adding the onions and ground beef, break up the meat with your hands. All of the ingredients should be fully combined. Divide the ingredients into equal quantities to make eight evenly sized balls. Form the balls into 34-inch patties that are 412 inches broad. Make a small divot in the center of each patty to keep the burgers from ballooning up on the grill.
The grates on the grill should be oiled. Grill the burgers under cover for 2 to 4 minutes, or until the first side is attractively browned. Burgers are turned over and cooked for a few minutes longer to get the desired amount of doneness. If desired, toast the buns on the cooler side of the grill before serving.

Nutrition Facts (1 portion):
Energy: 517Kcal
Carbs: 28g
Proteins: 38g
Fats: 27g

Carbs: 43g
Proteins: 40g
Fats: 25g

18. Burger with grilled onion

Portion Size: 2
Duration: 30 min

Ingredients:

2/4 lb. minced beef
2 hamburger buns split toasted
2/2 large sweet onion
Lettuce leaves
Tomato slices
Oil
pepper, salt; as desired

Instructions:
Create four ¾-inch-thick patties out of the ground beef by lightly forming them. Apply oil to the onion pieces.
On a grid over medium, ash-coated coals, arrange patties and onion slices. Cook covered over medium flame for 11 to 15 minutes (or 13 to 14 minutes on a preheated gas grill) or until an instant-read thermometer placed horizontally into the center reads 160 degrees F, flipping the food once. Grill onions for 10 to 12 minutes, or until they are soft, flipping them over halfway through.
Season the burgers and onions with salt and pepper to taste.
Place lettuce at the bottom of each bun. Burgers should be placed over lettuce. Add tomatoes and roasted onions on top. tight bun.

Nutrition Facts (1 portion):
Energy: 553Kcal

19. Homemade Beef Burger

Portion Size: 2
Duration: 35 min

Ingredients:

1 small egg beaten
½ onion, chopped
1 tsp olive oil
1x250g pack beef steak mince
½ tsp. mixed dried herbs
2 white rolls
Few round lettuces leave
½ beef tomato sliced

Instructions:

Add the onion to a frying pan with already-heated olive oil, and cook for 5 minutes, or until it softens and starts to become brown. Place aside.
Combine the egg, herbs, and beef mince in a bowl. After seasoning, add the onions and thoroughly combine. Shape into 2 patties using your hands.
On a warm grill or griddle, cook the burgers for 5 to 6 minutes on each side.
In the meantime, lightly grill the buns' cut sides. Place lettuce, hamburgers, and tomato slices within. If desired, top with ketchup while serving.

Nutrition Facts (1 portion):
Energy: 472Kcal
Carbs: 29g
Proteins: 32g
Fats: 26g

Fats: 33g

20. Zesty Onion Burger

Portion Size: 2
Duration: 35 min

Ingredients:

1/2 lb. of beef mince
1 cup of sliced celery
1/2 can of blended condensed onion soup
1/8 cup of water
1/8 cups of ketchup
1/2 a tsp Worcestershire sauce
1/8 tsp mustard
1/8 tsp pepper
three hamburger buns split
one Tbsp softened butter

Instructions:

Sauté the beef and celery in a container. Next, drain. Put the ketchup, mustard, Worcestershire, pepper, soup, and water in it. The mixture should quickly come to a boil. Simmer until the mixture has thickened, stirring occasionally.
Toast the buns after buttering the sliced sides. Add a meat mixture on top.

Nutrition Facts (1 portion):
Energy: 683Kcal
Carbs: 64g
Proteins: 34g

21. Chicken Chili Burger

Portion Size: 2
Duration: 45 min

Ingredients:

1 1/2 lb. of chicken cutlets
1/4 of a bell pepper, cut finely
3 Tbsp chili sauce oil, for grill rack
Part-skim sharp cheddar cheese, eight slices
2 hamburgers buns
1/4 large red onion, slices
2 leaves of lettuce

Instructions:

If using cutlets, rinse and dry the chicken. After cutting into 2-inch pieces and processing in a food processor, transfer to a bowl once roughly crushed. Crumble some ground chicken into a bowl if using. The same recipe can now be used to make both chicken cutlets and ground chicken.
Season the chicken with salt and pepper.
Blend the bell pepper, cilantro, and chili sauce with your hands rapidly; do not overmix.
Form into two 1 1/2-inch-thick patties.
Start the grill. Lightly oil the rack.
Grill the burgers for 5 minutes on a rack over medium heat.
After flipping the burgers, top each with a slice of cheese. Grill the burgers for another 5 minutes, or until well done.
Cook the buns with the sliced side down for a minute, or until golden brown.

Fill buns with lettuce, onion, and hamburgers.

Nutrition Facts (1 portion):
Energy: 576Kcal
Carbs: 64g
Proteins: 25g
Fats: 22g

22. Chicken Parmesan Burger

Portion Size: 2
Duration: 35 min

Ingredients:

2 burger Buns
1/4 cup of parmesan cheese, finely grated
2 Tbsp basil, chopped
3/4 cup of marinara sauce
6 oz of white flesh chicken ground
1 tbsp olive oil
1/2 Tbsps. grated onion
2 oz of thinly sliced whole-milk mozzarella cheese and 1/8 tsp salt
2 substantial radish leaves

Instructions:

Finely chop the Parmesan and bread dice in a food processor. Before transferring to the pie plate, stir in 2 tablespoons minced basil.
Combine marinara and two tablespoons basil in a small pot. 1 1/2 tablespoons sauce should be added to a large mixing bowl. Mix in the chicken, onion, 1/2 cup oil, and 1/4 teaspoon salt. Add the pepper and mix well. Form into two 1/2-inch-thick patties. Crumble it up. Warm the sauce over low heat.
Warm 1 12 tbsp oil in a large nonstick skillet over medium heat. Patties should be cooked for 4 minutes, or until the bottoms are crispy. Flip the burgers over and top with cheese. Cooking time is 3 minutes. Cook for 1 minute, or until thoroughly cooked and the cheese has melted, covered. To make burgers, combine bread, radicchio, basil leaves, and warm marinara.

Nutrition Facts (1 portion):
Energy: 554Kcal
Carbs: 38g
Proteins: 35g
Fats: 28g

23. Zeus Burger

Portion Size: 2
Duration: 35 min

Ingredients:
1 1/2 tbsp. of fat-free mayonnaise
1/2 tsp minced garlic
Dried oregano, 1/8 tsp., a dash of salt
lean ground beef, half a pound
Splitting two hamburger buns
2 tbsp. of thawed and squeezed-dry chopped frozen spinach
Reduced-fat feta cheese, 2 Tbsps., crumbled
1 tsp lemon juice
pine nuts, cut into one tsp
1/2 tsps. garlic & dried oregano
Salt, 1/8tsp
half tsp of pepper

Instructions:
Combine the salt, oregano, garlic, lemon juice, and mayonnaise in a small mixing basin. Refrigerate until ready to serve.
In a large mixing bowl, combine the spinach, cheese, lemon juice, pine nuts, oregano, salt, and pepper. Stir in the crumbled beef to the stew. By shaping, create two patties.
Using long-handled tongs, coat the grill rack with cooking oil on a paper towel. Cook for 5-7 minutes each side on a covered grill over medium heat, or until a meat thermometer reads 160° and the juices flow, or under a grill positioned 4 inches from the heat.

After 1 minute of grilling, the buns should be lightly browned. Serve the burgers with the sauce you saved on buns.

Nutrition Facts (1 portion):
Energy: 425 Kcal
Carbs: 40 g
Proteins: 33 g
Fats: 14 g

24. Greek Style chicken burger

Portion Size: 2
Duration: 35 min

Ingredients:

1/2 pounds of shredded chicken
1/6 cup of dry, fine breadcrumbs
1/2 egg
1 tbsp. milk
Lime juice, half a Tbsp
1/8 tsps. of salt & pepper
1 tbsp. of vegetable oil
2 burger buns
Mayonnaise (exclusively for use inside burgers)
2 red onions, sliced
2 tomatoes, sliced
2 leaves green leaf lettuce

Instructions:

Mix the salt, chicken, egg, pepper, lemon juice, bread crumbs, and milk in a container. The mixture is divided into two patties.
A big nonstick skillet should be heated to a moderately high temperature for the oil. Once they are light brown and less pink inside, patties should be cooked for approximately eight minutes.

Spread mayonnaise inside the burger bun, then add the cooked Patti, a tomato slice, a lettuce leaf, and a slice of red onion. Let's enjoy ourselves.

Nutrition Facts (1 portion):
Energy: 382 Kcal
Carbs: 32 g
Proteins: 28 g
Fats: 14 g

25. Cheddar Chicken burger

Portion Size: 2
Duration: 20 min

Ingredients:

1/2 pound of ground chicken
1 clove of garlic
1/2 spoonful of Worcestershire sauce
1/4 cup diced, cheddar cheese
1/2 Tbsp canola oil
2 hamburger buns
The toppings of your preference

Instructions:
With the exception of the oil, combine all of the ingredients in a mixing bowl and toss to combine. Don't mix too much.
Patties should be 2 inches thick. Make every effort to evenly distribute the cheddar cubes. (Note: The mixture holds together while being damp. It's a good idea to moisten your hands before making the patties. Heat the oil in a large skillet over medium-high heat. Heat the oil in a large skillet over medium-high heat. Cook the hamburgers in the heated skillet for 5 minutes. When fully cooked, flip over and cook for another five minutes. (When flipping the burgers, just cut down the heat a little if your stove is getting too hot. Add your extra slices

of cheddar now if you want to top these burgers with it.)

Place patties on a platter and let aside for 5 minutes before serving.

Serve in a bun with your choice burger toppings.

Nutrition Facts (1 portion):
Energy: 270Kcal
Carbs: 3g
Proteins: 25g
Fats: 18g

Pork

1. Pork Chops

Portion Size: 2
Duration: 40 min

Ingredients:

1 pork chop
1/10 tsp of chicken seasoning
1/10 cup melted butter
8 oz of salve of mushrooms soup in a ¼ -can
1/2 Tbsp of chopped, frozen onions
1/8 cup milk
1/10 cup of water

Instructions:

Pork chops are pan-browned in melted butter on one side.
Turn over after adding the remaining Ingredients.
Simmer for about 60 minutes.

Nutrition Facts (1 portion):

Energy: 60 Kcal
Carbs:1.3g
Proteins: 0.11 g
Fats 5.9g

2. Pork loin crunch in red wine

Portion Size: 2
Duration: 40 min

Ingredients:

1 pound. roast pork loin
1/4 tbsp. Basil
1/4 of a tsp of pepper powder
1/4 of a tsp of minced fresh garlic
1/4 of a tsp nutmeg
1/8 cup red wine
1/5 cup of olive oil
 water
1/4 cup bran flakes, optionally with raisins (cereal)

Instructions:

Combine the garlic and dry Ingredients.
Use to coat the roast.
Crush cereal in the bag, then push or pat it into the roast, or roll the roast in the cereal.
Place in a roasting pan that is 9 x 13 and has been drizzled with olive oil to assist prevent sticking.
At this point, add wine and water to the pan for the roast.
Cover with tin foil tent style.
Depending on the oven, bake for 1 1/2 to 2 hours at 350°F.
(Remove tin foil 15 minutes before serving to create a crusty covering).
Slice into one piece.
Drippings can be used to glaze the meat.
This produces an extremely rich au jus sauce.

Nutrition Facts (1 portion):

Energy: 398Kcal
Carbs: 5.47g
Proteins: 54g
Fats: 15.5g

3. Pork Taquitos

Portion Size: 2
Duration: 50 min

Ingredients:
1/6 of a medium onion, minced
1/6 Tbsp canola oil
minced 1/3 of the garlic cloves
⅓ tsp of cumin powder
one-six tsp ground chili
a dash of cayenne pepper
1/3 cup pork, cooked and shredded
Shredded Mexican cheese mixture, 1/6 cup (4 oz.).
1/10 cup freshly minced cilantro
1/10 cup Verde salsa
2 warmed 6-inch corn tortillas

Instructions:
In a large skillet, sauté the onion in oil until tender. After adding the cayenne, chili powder, and garlic, cook for one minute more. Salsa, cheese, c lantro, and shredded pork should all be included. Cook and whisk the cheese to melt it.

Spread 2 tablespoons of filling on the bottom third of each tortilla. Roll tightly. To fasten, use toothpicks. Fill the remaining tortillas in the same way.

Place the taquitos on a greased baking sheet. Bake for 8 minutes at 400°. Allow it to cool completely. Remove the toothpicks. Line a baking sheet 15 inches by 10 inches by 1 inch with wax paper and place the taquitos on it. Freeze until completely solid. Fill a freezer bag that can be sealed with plastic. Perhaps frozen for three months.

When using frozen tacos, place the needed number of tacos in a single layer on a preheated baking sheet. Bake for 12 to 15 minutes at 400° until golden brown. Garnish with sour cream.

Nutrition Facts (1 portion):
Energy: 197Kcal
Carbs: 13g
Proteins: 12g
Fats: 11

4. Pork tenderloin stir fry with Tangerines

Portion Size: 2
Duration: 25 min

Ingredients:
5/8 pound trimmed, crosswise-cut pork tenderloin
1/2 Tbsps. corn flour
1 Tbsp of Asian sesame oil, split
Fresh ginger, peeled and chopped, 1/2 tbsp.
2 unpeeled clementines, diced
2 Tbsps. of chili sauce
1 Tbsp soy sauce
1/8 tsp Chinese five-spice powder
3 baby Bok choy, diced
2 ½ thinly sliced onion

Instructions:
Place the pork tenderloin strips in a container and coat with corn flour after seasoning with pepper and salt. Heat 1 tbsp sesame oil in a large nonstick skillet. After adding the minced ginger, stir for 30 seconds.

Fry the pork strips for three minutes, or until they are almost done and starting to brown. Mix in the tangerine chunks for 30 seconds. Add soy sauce, five-spice powder, and sweet chili sauce to taste. Boil for a minute, stirring regularly, until the sauce in the skillet begins to thicken gradually.

Add the Bok choy, half of the sliced green onions, and the last tablespoon of sesame oil. Bok choy should be stir-fried for a few seconds, or until wilted. Season with pepper and salt to taste.

Nutrition Facts (1 portion):
Energy: 253 Kcal
Carbs: 7.6g
Proteins: 37g
Fats: 9.6g

5. Pulled pork sandwich

Portion Size: 2
Duration: 30 min

Ingredients:

6 oz of cooked and shredded pork
Reduced sodium chicken broth, half a cup
1 Tbsp balsamic vinegar
1 Tbsp of brown sugar
1/2 tsp Chili powder
1/2 tsp Paprika
1/2 tsp crushed cumin
a dash of salt
1/8 tsp black pepper, ground
2 Kaiser rolls, cut in half

Instructions:

Mix the pork with the chicken broth, pepper, sugar, cumin, salt, chili powder, and vinegar, and paprika in a medium pot.
Have it simmer.
Stir until the sauce thickens and the liquid has decreased.
Serve pork on halved Kaiser rolls.

Nutrition Facts (1 portion):

Energy: 458 kcal
Carbs: 37g
Proteins: 28g
Fats: 20g

6. Pork sausage gravy

Portion Size: 2
Duration: 30 min

Ingredients:

1/2 lb. Fresh, ground pork sausage
1/2 cups milk, or as required
1/5 cup all-purpose flour,
salt, and pepper as desired

Instructions:

In a wok, crumble, and brown sausage. Take out of the skillet, then set aside.
Mix in 1/2 to 1 cup of flour while whisking the remaining drippings. Verify that all of the drips have been absorbed.
Add milk gradually until the mixture is creamy. Top with the pepper, cooked sausage, and salt to taste.

Nutrition Facts (1 portion):

Energy: 408Kcal
Carbs: 11g
Proteins: 20g
Fats: 30g

7. Pork Sausage with lentils

Portion Size: 2
Duration: 45 min

Ingredients:
1/2 a cup of olive oil
2 oz. diced pancetta
1 finely chopped yellow onion
6 pieces of pork sausage
4 oz of mushrooms and 2 finely minced garlic cloves
3/4 cups of brown lentils and one cup of chopped basil
1/4 of a cup of white wine
1 cup of canned chicken broth
1 cup baby spinach leaves
freshly crushed black pepper and salt to taste.

Instructions:
In a large sauté pan (ideally nonstick), heat the oil and cook the pancetta until it is crispy. Using a slotted spoon, remove the pancetta and place it in a basin.
In a pan, sauté the onions until soft but not browned. Remove the onions with a slotted spoon and place them in the bowl with the pancetta. Sausages are added, the heat is decreased to medium, and they are browned all over. Return the pancetta and onions to the pan. Before adding the garlic, mushrooms, basil, and lentils to the pan, carefully combine everything. Increase the heat to medium-high, then add the consommé and bring to a boil. The white wine is added, the heat is reduced to medium, and the pot is covered for 25 minutes to simmer. Baby spinach leaves have been inserted. Season with salt and freshly ground black pepper to taste.
In shallow plates, serve with fresh bread rolls.

Nutrition Facts (1 portion):
Energy: 1440Kcal
Carbs: 56g
Proteins: 85g
Fats: 85g

8. Pork Chops and apple bake

Portion Size: 2
Duration: 70 min

Ingredients:
2 pork chops, around 3/4 inch thick
2/5 cup wheat germ
2/5 egg
2/5 tsp of garlic powder and basil
2/5 tsp rosemary
4/5 Tbsps. balsamic vinegar
2/5 tsp cinnamon
Apple, one
1/5 cup water
pepper, salt; as desired

Instructions:
In a mixing dish, whisk together the eggs.
In a separate bowl, combine the wheat germ, rosemary, basil, and garlic powder. Rinse and dry pork chops (which could be pork loin chops or pork steaks). Brush the chops with the egg wash. Dredge the wheat germ mixture. Fill a 9x13 roasting pan halfway with water. Drizzle with balsamic vinegar to finish. Preheat the oven to 350°F for 12 hours. Meanwhile, remove the apple's cores and quarter it. In another basin, combine cinnamon. Swirl the mixture around the apple in the basin. After half an hour, flip the chops and top with apples. Return them to the oven and bake for another 15 minutes.
NOTE: Check for doneness after 1 hour of total baking time, depending on the thickness of the chops and oven variations. There is a time range of one to one and a half hours.
Serve with veggies and a vegetable side dish.

Nutrition Facts (1 portion):
Energy: 168Kcal
Carbs: 30g
Proteins: 6.6g
Fats: 3.7 g

9. Pork Stew

Portion Size: 2
Duration: 30 min

Ingredients:

9/10 lbs. pork steak,
1/2 large sweet onions, cubed
1 large carrot
1/2 cups hewed celery
1/8 (4 oz.) can of tomato paste
1 minced garlic clove and 1/2 tbsp. base mushroom stock
1 cup of water
1/2 Tbsp of olive oil
1/4 of a fresh rosemary sprig, salt, and pepper

Instructions:

In a large stock pot, fry pork cubes in batches until golden brown. Separate the juices and set them aside.
Cook the onion in the pan with the olive oil for 5 to 6 minutes, or until softened and beginning to color. After adding the garlic, carrots, and celery, stir them in. Stir in the tomato paste and stock base until the vegetables are coated evenly.
Add water after putting the pork in the pan with any juices. Remember to include the rosemary sprig.
Boil, stirring frequently, for two to three hours on low heat.

Nutrition Facts (1 portion):

Energy: 329Kcal
Carbs: 14g
Proteins: 41g
Fats: 11 g

10. Pork Chow Mein

Portion Size: 2
Duration: 20 min

Ingredients:

2/3 Tbsp vegetable oil
1/2 cups sliced onions & celery
2/3 cups cooked pork, diced
1 tbsp. soy sauce
5 1/3 oz. bean sprouts drained
1 tbsp. cornstarch
2/3 cups beef broth
boiled rice

Instructions:

In a deep pan, heat the oil.
For five minutes, sauté the onion and celery.
add meat, soy sauce, and sprouts to the mixture.
Stir-fry for two minutes.
Combine the broth and corn flour.
Stirring continuously until it reaches boiling point, add to the skillet.
Three more minutes of cooking are required.
Eat with noodles or rice.

Nutrition Facts (1 portion):

Energy: 335Kcal
Carbs: 11g
Proteins: 25g
Fats: 21g

11. Skillet pork chops with carrot and pearl onion

Portion Size: 2
Duration: 25 min

Ingredients:

1/2 tsp of canola oil
2 center-cut, 6 oz. pork chops, with the bone in
1/2 tsp of salt
1 cup of carrots, diagonally sliced
6 oz or half a cup of thawed frozen pearl onions
1 tsp of multi-purpose flour
1/2 cup of unsalted chicken stock
1 tsp of Dijon mustard
½ a tsp Black pepper
1 Tbsp of chopped, unsalted butter

Instructions:

Heat the oil in a pan.
Sprinkle ½ tsp of salt over the pork chops. After three minutes on each side, the pork should be well-browned. Remove the pork from the pan and set aside.
Cook the carrots and onions for about 3 minutes, stirring often.
Cook the flour in the skillet for 30 seconds, stirring often. Bring the stock and mustard to a boil in a skillet. Simmer, covered, for 5 minutes, stirring often.
Replace the meat in the skillet and cover with the liquid. Add pepper and the remaining 1/8 teaspoon salt. Simmer the meal with the lid on for 2 to 3 minutes when the sauce has slightly thickened, the pork is well heated, and the carrots are soft. After removing from the fire, drizzle with butter.

Nutrition Facts (1 portion):

Energy: 297 Kcal
Carbs: 13g
Proteins: 33g
Fats: 11g

12. Garlic Lime Pork with spinach

Portion Size: 2
Duration: 30 min

Ingredients:

1 Tbsp of lime juice
1/2 Tbsp almond or peanut butter
2 minced garlic cloves
pepper, salt; as desired
1 tsp. honey
2 (8-oz) bone-in pork chops, chopped
2 tsp of olive oil
1 packet (2 oz) of fresh baby spinach

Instructions:

In a mixing bowl, combine the pepper, lime juice, salt, peanut butter, honey, and garlic. The last 1/8 teaspoon of salt and pepper should be sprinkled over the chops. Warm 2 tablespoons oil in a pan. Add the chops and cook for 7 to 10 minutes, rotating once. Remove from the skillet; cover and keep heated.
Warm the remaining two tablespoons of oil in the same skillet over medium-low heat. Before adding the lime mixture, whisk to remove any browned, crusty bits. Sauté and stir the spinach until it is well cooked and begins to wilt. Season with additional pepper if desired.
Chops should be served. Serve with lime wedges and walnuts, if desired.

Nutrition Facts (1 portion):

Energy: 352Kcal
Carbs: 25g
Proteins: 37g
Fats: 11g

13. Pork Chops with Garlicky Broccoli

Portion Size: 2
Duration: 30 min

Ingredients:

1 lb. of spear-shaped, trimmed, broccoli with stems
3 Tbsp olive oil
1/2 cup panko breadcrumbs, preferably whole-wheat
1/8 cup finely crushed Parmesan cheese
1/8 cup flour from whole wheat
1 single, slightly beat small egg.
2 (2 oz) trimmed, boneless pork chops
1/4 tsps. of salt & red pepper
2 finely sliced garlic cloves
red wine vinegar, 1 tbsp.

Instructions:

After turning the grill to high, position the rack in the upper third of the oven. Line a baking sheet with foil and set aside. After tossing the broccoli with 1 tablespoon of oil, arrange it in an even layer in the heated skillet. Broil for about 10 minutes, stirring occasionally, until some sections are blackened. After transferring, place in a basin. Meanwhile, in a shallow dish, combine the Parmesan and breadcrumbs. In a third shallow dish, combine the egg and flour. The pork should be seasoned with 1/8 teaspoon salt before being coated in flour and bread crumbs. 1 tablespoon oil in a large nonstick skillet over medium-high heat. Cook until the pork is golden brown and an instant-read thermometer inserted into the thickest section reads 145 degrees F. Cook the meat for about 6 minutes total, flipping once.
 Serve on a platter with lemon juice. Cover it with foil. Clean out the pan. Cook the remaining 1 tsp oil, garlic, and crushed red pepper over low heat, stirring regularly, for 3 minutes, or until the garlic is sizzling. After pulling the pan off the heat, add the vinegar and the remaining 1/2 teaspoon salt. Coat the broccoli with the drizzle. Top the broccoli and meat with more Parmesan cheese if desired.

Nutrition Facts (1 portion):

Energy: 543 Kcal
Carbs: 21g
Proteins: 34g
Fats: 37g

14. Pork Pot Pie

Portion Size: 2
Duration: 40 min

Ingredients:

1 medium carrot, cut thin
1/2 small onion, chopped
1/8cup of water
1 cup of cooked pork cubes
1/2 can, cream of celery soup
1 tbsp finely chopped fresh parsley
1/8tsp of salt
1/8tsp of garlic powder
A 9-inch single-crust pie's worth of pastry
½ of crushed parmesan cheese

Instructions:

Cook the carrots and onion in water in a saucepan until soft; drain. Add the soup, pork, parsley, salt, savory, and garlic powder. Transfer to a 9-inch pie pan that has been buttered. Roll out the pastry into a 10-inch. circle and set it over the meat mixture on a lightly dusted surface. Make slits at the top and flute the edges. Add a little Parmesan cheese. To achieve golden brown results, bake for 18 to 20 minutes, at 425°. before cutting, let stand for five minutes.

Nutrition Facts (1 portion):

Energy: 609Kcal
Carbs: 25g
Proteins: 34g
Fats: 40g

15. Pork Rice Stir-Fry

Portion Size: 2
Duration: 20 min

Ingredients:

2 oz. pork tenderloin, diced
2 tsp. canola oil
1/4 cup sliced fresh mushroom
¼ cup Fresh sugar snap peas
1 Tbsp diced red sweet pepper and green pepper
1/2 tbsp. hewed onion (green)
1/8tsp garlic, minced
1/2 Tbsp soy sauce
1/8tsp, of sugar
1/2 cup of leftover rice

Instructions:
Fry the pork in two Tbsps. of oil in a big pan for between three and five mins. Take it off and keep warm. Leftover oil should be warmed in the very same pan. Add the water chestnuts, peas, peppers, onions, mushrooms, and garlic after the vegetables are crisp-tender.
Soy sauce and sugar should be combined, then added to the vegetable combination. Cook for two mins. Back the pork into the pan. Stir in the rice after adding it. Cook for 5 mins, or until thoroughly cooked.

Nutrition Facts (1 portion):

Energy: 184Kcal
Carbs: 22 g
Proteins: 9.6g
Fats: 6.3g

16. BBQ Pork Chops

Portion Size: 2
Duration: 100 min

Ingredients:

1/3 of a pork chop
1/3 of a Spanish onion
1 tbsp. of brown sugar
1/8 cup of ketchup
¼ cups of water

Instructions:

With a thick slice of Spanish onion on top, for about five minutes each, grill the pork chops on both sides. On top of each pork chop, sprinkle brown sugar.
2/3 cups water should be added to 1/3 cup of ketchup.
Cover the pork chops after pouring the mixture over them.
Bake covered for about an hour at 350 degrees. After that, bake uncovered for an additional 30 minutes.

Nutrition Facts (1 portion):

Energy: 88Kcal
Carbs: 11g
Proteins: 0.78g
Fats: 4.16g

17. Shredded Pork Tacos

Portion Size: 2
Duration: 170 min

Ingredients:

1/2 lbs. of pork loin
1 garlic clove, minced
1 tsp cumin
1/4 cup minced onion
Apple cider vinegar, half Tbsp
½ tbsp. olive oil
1 Tbsps. of pureed chipotle chilies in adobo
1/8 cup finely chopped fresh cilantro
1 Tbsp of water

Instructions:

In the crock pot, mix all the ingredients in no particular sequence, and simmer for 3 hrs., or until done.
When the pork is thoroughly cooked, shred it and serve it with your preferred toppings on warm tortillas.

Nutrition Facts (1 portion):

Energy: 312Kcal
Carbs: 3.4g
Proteins: 24g
Fats: 10g

18. Chinese pork tenderloin

Portion Size: 2
Duration: 45 min

Ingredients:

Trimmed 2/3 pork tenderloins
2 tsp light soy sauce
Sherry, 1/3 cup
1 tsp Black bean sauce
½ tsp. ginger fresh, minced
1/2 tsp. brown sugar in a bag
1/3 of a garlic clove
1/6 tsp. sesame oil
Chinese five-spice powder, 1/3 of a pinch

Instructions:

In a small glass dish, arrange the tenderloins. Mix the black bean sauce, soy sauce, sherry, ginger, sugar, garlic, sesame oil, and five-spice powder in a small bowl. Pour the marinade over the pork, turning it to coat. Refrigerate for up to 24 hours or at least two hours with a cover on.
The oven should be heated at 375 degrees F. While the oven is preheating, remove the tenderloins from the refrigerator.
Pork should be baked in a preheated oven for 30 to 35 minutes, or until the desired doneness. After 10 minutes, slice thinly in a diagonal motion.

Nutrition Facts (1 portion):

Energy: 195Kcal
Carbs: 4.6g
Proteins: 35g
Fats: 3.5g

19. BBQ Pulled Tuna Sandwich

Portion Size: 2
Duration: 20 min

Ingredients:

1/4 of cup of red onion slices
1 clove of garlic
1/2 tbsp. water, or more as necessary
Pork in 1 1/2 (6 oz.) cans, drained
1/2 tsp, Worcestershire sauce
1/2 tbsp of steak spice
1/2 cup barbeque sauce
1/8 cup butter
2 substantial soft rolls, warmed

Instructions:

Cook and whisk the water, onion, and garlic for 5 mins, or till the ingredients are soft. Worcestershire sauce, tuna, and steak seasoning should all be added. Stir in the barbecue sauce. Allow the flavors to meld for about 5 minutes while simmering on low heat.
On soft rolls, butter them. Serve the rolls with the tuna mixture heaped on top.

Nutrition Facts (1 portion):

Energy: 252Kcal
Carbs: 25g
Proteins: 13g
Fats: 11g

20. Pork sandwich spread

Portion Size: 2
Duration: 15 min

Ingredients:

2/3 cup cooked ground pork
2 Tbsp minced celery and mayo
1/3 tbsp. of sweet pickle and coarsely chopped onion
pepper, to taste,
1/3 tbsp. prepared mustard
4 slices white bread

Instructions:

Stir the first seven ingredients in a container. About 1-1/3 cups of the mixture should be distributed over both the two pieces of bread, followed by the final slice of bread.

Nutrition Facts (1 portion):

Energy: 503Kcal
Carbs: 27g
Proteins: 27g
Fats: 31g

21. Pork Sausage patties

Portion Size: 2
Duration: 30 min

Ingredients:

1/3 beaten egg
1/8 cup of milk
2 Tbsp finely minced onion
2/3 Tbsp multipurpose unbleached flour
a dash of salt and a sprinkle of pepper
1 lb. of bulk sage pork sausage

Instructions:

Combine the first six Ingredients in the big vessel. Stir thoroughly after adding the banger crumbs to the batter.
Form into six patties.
Cook patties, flipping once or twice, in a pan for six mins on each side.

Nutrition Facts (1 portion):

Energy: 32.6Kcal
Carbs: 4.1 g
Proteins: 1.7 g
Fats: 0.33g

22. Pork Sausage and apple patties

Portion Size: 2
Duration: 30 min

Ingredients:

1/4 coarsely sliced apple
1/2 cup of breadcrumbs
1/4 cup coarsely sliced celery
1 tbsp brown sugar
1/2 pounds of bulk pork sausage

Instructions:

Combine all ingredients, then shape into patties.
Bake at 350° F for 30 minutes while covered.
Bake for 10 more minutes with the cover off.
Note: If wanted, you can bake some extra apples, covered, at the same time the patties, in 1/4-inch-thick rings, with a little sugar sprinkled on top. Each burger should be served on an apple ring.

Nutrition Facts (1 portion):

Energy: 433Kcal
Carbs: 19g
Proteins: 27g
Fats: 26g

23. Pork Chops and bean Bake

Portion Size: 2
Duration: 60 min

Ingredients:

2/3 can of tomato beans
1 2/3 lean pork chops
2 Tbsps. of brown sugar
2 Tbsp ketchup
5 to 6 slices of an onion
5 to 6 thin slices of lemon
fresh milled black pepper, salt

Instructions:

In a baking dish measuring 13x9x2, put the beans.
Place chops over beans.
Add pepper and salt as per preference.
Apply mustard to chops sparingly.
Add some brown sugar on top.
Spread ketchup on.
Bake for 1 1/4 hours at 325 F with the lid off.
Place a piece of onion and lemon on each chop.
Bake for 15 minutes.

Nutrition Facts (1 portion):

Energy: 252Kcal
Carbs: 56g
Proteins: 8.24g
Fats: 1.51g

24. Pork Lo Mein

Portion Size: 2
Duration: 20 min

Ingredients:

1/2 pounds of pork tenderloin
1/8cup soy sauce (low sodium)
1 1/2 minced garlic cloves
1 tsp fresh ginger, chopped
1/8tsp red pepper flakes
1 cup of fresh snow peas,
1/2 medium sized red pepper
1/2 cup cooked thin spaghetti
3 Tbsp of chicken broth with reduced sodium
1 tsp sesame oil

Instructions:

Tenderloin should be cut in half lengthwise. Set aside each half after slicing it into 1/4-inch-thick slices. Pork is combined with soy sauce, garlic, ginger, and pepper flakes in a large, sealable plastic bag. Refrigerate for 20 minutes after sealing and coating the bag.
Place the pork in a large nonstick skillet coated with frying spray and cook for 4-5 minutes, or until the flesh is no longer pink. For one minute, stir-fry the peas and red pepper. Cook for another minute after adding the noodles and broth. After the heat is turned off, add the sesame oil.

Nutrition Facts (1 portion):

Energy: 367Kcal
Carbs: 42g
Proteins: 35g
Fats: 5.59g

25. Pork Jerky

Portion Size: 2
Duration: 30 min

Ingredients:

8 3/4 oz of pork mince
1 Tbsp fish sauce
2 Tbsps. rose wine
1 Tbsps. soy sauce
1/2 Tbsp dark soy sauce
1/4 cups. of sugar

Instructions:

Stir the aforementioned ingredients into the pork mince until a mixture is formed. Refrigerate for two hours to improve flavor.

Place the pork mince in the center of the aluminum foil and cover with a plastic sheet or wrap. Gently flatten the mince with your hand.

Then, using a rolling pin, lightly flatten the mince to equalize the meat's thickness and improve the grill's impact. See Figure Remove the plastic baking sheet, preheat the oven to 300°F, and then transfer the meat and aluminum foil to a baking tray. Bake the meat in the center of the oven for 12 minutes. After 12 minutes, remove the tray; the gravy will be there; set it aside. Place the meat on a higher rack in the oven. Cook the meal for an additional 8 to 10 minutes, or until it begins to take on a charcoal-like look, after switching the oven's heat setting from bake to grill. Remove the grilled meat and allow it to cool before slicing it into thin strips.

Nutrition Facts (1 portion):

Energy: 242Kcal
Carbs: 16g
Proteins: 27g
Fats: 7.5g

26. Pork Loin Stuffed with Spinach

Portion Size: 2
Duration: 150 min

Ingredients:

1/5 (10 oz.) container of thawed and drained frozen chopped spinach
Margarine, 1/4 of a cup
1/8 cup dry bread crumbs
1/5 cup sliced onion
1 Pork tenderloin, 1/4 pound
Ketchup, ⅗ tbsp.
4/5 tbsp. teriyaki sauce
Ground cumin, 1/5 tsp
1 garlic clove

Instructions:

Preheat the oven to 350 degrees Fahrenheit. Sauté spinach, butter, onions, and garlic in a skillet over medium heat until soft. I'll top it with bread crumbs. Cut the tenderloin in half lengthwise. After stuffing with spinach mixture, secure with kitchen thread.

In a mixing bowl, combine teriyaki sauce and ketchup. Half-baste the tenderloin with the mixture. Cook the meat with cumin. Place in a deep roaster and roast for an hour, uncovered, at 350°F. Cook, covered, for another hour while basting with the reserved marinade. On an instant-read thermometer, the interior temperature should be 145 degrees Fahrenheit.

Nutrition Facts (1 portion):

Energy: 432Kcal
Carbs: 12 g
Proteins: 59g
Fats: 14g

Proteins: 29g
Fats: 22g

27. Pork chop with creamy mushroom sauce

Portion Size: 2
Duration: 30 min
Ingredients:
2 bone-in pork chops, trimmed, one pound, 1/2-3/4 inch thick
a pinch of salt
1/4 tsp of pepper
1 1/2 tsp olive oil
1/4 cup of shallots, minced
4 oz of sliced mixed mushrooms,
1/4 cup dry white wine
1/4 cup of fresh parsley, minced

Instructions:

Season the pork chops with 1/4 teaspoon salt and pepper. 1 Tbsp oil, ideally cast iron, in a large skillet over medium-high heat. Reduce the heat to medium and add two pork chops. Cook for 5 to 7 minutes, flipping once, or until thoroughly cooked. Cover with foil and place on a plate.
Add another tablespoon of oil to the pan. When the mushrooms have browned, about 2 to 4 minutes, add the shallots and continue to cook, stirring frequently. Continue simmering, scraping out any browned parts, for 1 to 3 minutes, or until the liquid has mostly evaporated, after adding the wine and the final 1/4 teaspoon of salt. Herbs are added and simmered for about another minute, or until bubbling. Chops should be accompanied by mushroom sauce.

Nutrition Facts (1 portion):

Energy: 357 Kcal
Carbs: 6g

28. Pork and green bean stir-fry

Portion Size: 2
Duration: 30 min

Ingredients:

1/8 cup of apricot jam
1 Tbsps. of soy sauce with a lower sodium content
1/2 Tbsps. of sesame oil
2 tsp of the Garlic-Chile sauce
Trimmed and thinly sliced 1/2-pound pork tenderloin
1/8 cup cornstarch
Grapeseed or avocado oil, 1 1/2 tsps.
6 oz of trimmed green beans
1/4 cup of scallions, finely sliced

Instructions:
Combine jam, soy sauce, sesame oil, and chili-garlic sauce in a small bowl. Set aside.
Combine corn flour and pork in a medium mixing bowl; stir until no corn flour is visible at the bottom of the bowl.
Grapeseed (or avocado) oil should be heated over high heat in a large flat-bottomed wok or cast-iron skillet until shimmering. After adding the pork, cook for 6 to 8 minutes, tossing frequently, until it is browned and crispy. At this time, add the green beans and simmer for 3 to 6 minutes, stirring frequently. Cook the jam mixture for 30 to 1 minute, stirring periodically, until fully coated. After removing from the heat, stir in the sesame seeds and scallions. Toss everything together. Top with more scallions if desired.

Nutrition Facts (1 portion):
Energy: 387 Kcal
Carbs: 29g

Proteins: 27g
Fats: 19g

Carbs: 80g
Proteins: 73g
Fats: 20g

29. Pork Butt Roast with Vegetable

Portion Size: 2
Duration: 70 min

Ingredients:

pepper and salt as desired
garlic powder to taste
1 1/2 lbs. of pork butt roast
5 raw potatoes
4 peeled carrots
1/2 onion
1/2 cup of mushrooms

Instructions:

Preheat the oven to 350 degrees F.
Melt the butter in a large frying pan over medium-high heat. After seasoning the pork on all sides, rub salt, pepper, and garlic powder into the flesh. All sides of the meat should be lightly browned. Place in a baking dish.
Place onion slices on top of the meat in the roasting pan. Fill the pan halfway with water. Place covered in a warm oven for three hours. Cook the potatoes and carrots for 45 minutes with the lid on. Cook for 15 minutes more after adding the mushrooms. Remove from the oven and set aside for at least 10 minutes before serving.

Nutrition Facts (1 portion):

Energy: 690Kcal

30. Pork Fried Rice

Portion Size: 2
Duration: 40 min

Ingredients:

3/8-inch chunks of 1/4 pound pork tenderloin
1 Tbsp of peanut oil
1/3 of a large white onion, chopped
Young peas, 1/3 cup, thawed if frozen
2 onions and 1/3 cup baby carrots, chopped
1/10 tsp of crushed red chili flakes
1 cup soy sauce
1 cup of rice, cooked

Instructions:

Heat the skillet.
Add Oil and stir to coat.
Cook the meat until the pink color has completely disappeared.
Saute the onion till translucent after adding it.
Put the Peas, Carrots, Soy Sauce, and Red Chile Flakes.
Vegetables should be stir-fried until they are crisp and tender.
Add rice and stir.

Nutrition Facts (1 portion):

Energy: 603 Kcal
Carbs: 108g
Proteins: 20g
Fats: 8.1g

To receive your FREE eBook

"Exclusive Argentine Asado recipes and delicious Turkish dishes"

Scan this QR Code

Poultry

1. Brown rice, Leek, and stir-fried chicken

Portion Size: 2
Duration: 55 min

Ingredients:

1/2 tbsp. olive oil
150g chicken breast, thinly slice
50g chorizo, chopped
1 leek, halved & finely sliced
1/2 red pepper, crushed
40g kale, leaves roughly chopped
½ tbsp. low salt soy sauces
1/2 tbsps. vinegar
250g pouches of microwave wholegrain rice

Instructions:

Cook the chicken in a hot pan with hot oil for three minutes. Combine with the chorizo. Cook for another 2 minutes, or until the chorizo fat has rendered and the chicken is gently browned. Using a fitted spoon, transfer the chicken and chorizo to a bowl while retaining as much oil from the pan as possible. Keep aside.
Add the leek and red pepper to the pan and cook for 2 minutes, stirring regularly. Cook for another minute, or until the edges of the kale are just beginning to wilt.
Add the rice, breaking it up with a wooden spoon, and then drizzle with the soy sauce and vinegar. After throwing the chicken and chorizo back in, toss everything together in the pan. After heating for 3 minutes, serve the rice.

Nutrition Facts (1 portion):

Energy: 398Kcal
Carbs: 33 g
Proteins: 26g
Fats: 16g

2. Baked Parmesan Cheese Chicken

Portion Size: 2
Duration: 35 min

Ingredients:

1 cup of parmesan cheese, shredded
1/2 tsp. of garlic powder.
1 tsp salt for celery
1 tsp. cayenne pepper
Skinless, boneless chicken thighs weighing 6 oz

Instructions:

Preheat the oven to 370°F. Wrap foil tightly around a jelly roll pan.
In a bowl, combine the olive oil. In a separate shallow bowl, combine the parmesan cheese, celery, pepper, and garlic powder.
Cut a chicken thigh in half. Chicken should be smeared with olive oil on both sides before pressing one side into the parmesan mixture to coat. Place the object, coated side up, on the prepared pan. Bake for about 25 minutes in a preheated oven. A thermometer inserted in the center should read at least 165°F

Nutrition Facts (1 portion):

Energy: 300Kcal
Carbs: 1g
Proteins: 28g
Fats: 22g

3. Chicken Vegetable Stew

Portion Size: 2
Duration: 35 min

Ingredients:

120 g chicken breasts
1 cups chicken broth
1 cubed potato
1/2 dice onion
1 minced garlic clove
1 diced carrot
¼ tsp. dried oregano and fresh dill
1 stalk celery
1 dash salt
¼ tsp. ground black pepper
¼ tsp. fresh rosemary chopped
1 bay leaves
1 tbsp. Olive oil

Instructions:

Add celery, carrots, onions, and garlic to some oil that has been heated at a moderate heat in a big pot.
Cook for three minutes. Add salt, oregano, rosemary, bay leaves, crushed black pepper, and chicken.
Combine everything and cook for a further 3 minutes. After that, incorporate the potatoes and chicken broth.
To cook the potatoes until they are soft, add an extra 17 to 18 minutes of cooking after bringing the ingredients to a boil.
After garnishing with dill, serve

Nutrition Facts (1 portion):

Energy: 775 Kcal
Carbs: 23 g
Proteins: 32 g
Fats: 62 g

4. Chicken curry

Portion Size: 2
Duration: 45 min

Ingredients:

1/2 lbs. boneless chicken breast
3/8 cup evaporated milk without fat
1 minced garlic clove
1/2 cup chopped mushrooms
1/2 cup. chicken bisque
1 carrot, cut and 1/8 large onion, chopped
½ tbsp. water
1/4 tsp curry powder
½ tsp cornstarch

Instructions:

Cook chicken for 30 minutes at 350 degrees, or until cooked through. When the chicken is safe to handle, chop it into bite-sized pieces. Combine chicken, broth, milk, curry, garlic, mushrooms, onions, and carrots in a soup pot. until it begins to boil, heat on a medium flame.
Stir the water and cornstarch. While stirring, slowly add the mixture. Add until the sauce becomes thick. Serve with rice.

Nutrition Facts (1 portion):

Energy: 183 Kcal
Carbs: 11 g
Proteins: 27 g
Fats: 3.4 g

5. Chicken Rice

Portion Size: 2
Duration: 25 min

Ingredients:

1 cup of water
1 cup freshly cut asparagus cut into diagonal segments of 1 inch
1/2 (6 oz.) package of rough and long grain rice blend
1/8 cup split low-fat butter
3/8 pound of 1-inch-wide slices of boneless, skinless chicken breast
Garlic, minced, 12 tsp.
1/2 medium carrot, shredded, and 1/8 tsp of salt
1 tbsps. Lime juice

Instructions:

In a hefty saucepan, blend the water, asparagus, and rice mix with the items of seasoning packet and 2 tbsp. butter. Reduce heat after bringing it to a boil. For 10 to 15 minutes, or until the water is absorbed, simmer the dish covered.
In the meantime, cook the chicken, garlic, and salt with the rest of butter in a large wok until the chicken juices run clear. Cook and swirl for one to two minutes, or until thoroughly cooked, before adding the carrot, lemon juice, and, if desired, lemon peel. Add to the rice mixture by stirring.

Nutrition Facts (1 portion):

Energy: 324Kcal
Carbs: 23g
Proteins: 28g
Fats: 15g

6. Lemon Herb Roast Chicken

Portion Size: 2
Duration: 15 min

Ingredients:

1/3 lemon
1/3 (10.75 oz.) can (98% fat-free) of Campbell's condensed cream of chicken soup
1/3 Tbsp freshly cut rosemary leaves
1/3 tbsp. freshly cut thyme leaves
1 minced garlic clove
1/3 (6 lb.) roasting a chicken
0.1 oz. of dry white wine
1/10 cup water

Instructions:

The oven is set to 375 degrees Fahrenheit. Grate one and a half teaspoons of lemon zest and squeeze one tablespoon of lemon juice.
In a normal mixing basin, combine the soup, rosemary, thyme, and garlic with the lemon juice, zest, and other herbs. 1 cup of the soup mixture should be set aside for the gravy. Fill a small roasting pan halfway with chicken.
Roast the chicken for 20 minutes. Brush the chicken with 1/4 cup of the soup mixture.
Cook for 1 hour and 15 minutes, or until the chicken is done. Transfer the chicken to a serving platter and keep it warm.
Using a spoon, remove any fat from the pan juices. Stir the wine in the roasting pan over a medium-high heat and bring it to a boil, scraping the brown pieces from the bottom of the pan. When the mixture is hot and boiling, add the water and the soup mixture you set aside. Serve the gravy alongside the chicken.

Nutrition Facts (1 portion):

Energy: 112 Kcal
Carbs: 2.57 g
Proteins: 13 g

Fats: 3.82 g

Fats: 19g

7. Chicken Bhuna Masala

Portion Size: 2
Duration: 35 min

Ingredients:

1 tsp. cumin seeds
1 tsps. of coriander seeds
1 Tbsp of vegetable oil
1 chicken breast that has been raw and cubed, salt, and freshly ground black pepper
12 a cinnamon stick
2 large tomatoes, diced; one-half of red onion; 2 garlic cloves; and one tsp of fresh ginger, chopped.
1 tsp of curry &chili powder
1/3 cup coconut milk, 1/3 cup
1/3 cup of white wine
1 cup of cooked basmati rice

Instructions:

Cook the coriander, cumin and cardamom in a large skillet over low heat for about a minute or until you can smell the spices. Utilizing a spice grinder, carefully grind the spices. When the oil is very hot or smoking, add it to the skillet and heat it over medium-high. Add the chicken and salt and pepper to taste. Before combining, let the chicken brown completely on either side. Add the remaining ground spices, white wine, tomatoes, onion, garlic, ginger, chili powder, curry powder, cinnamon, and coconut milk. Heat to come to a boil then reduce heat and simmer for an hour to thicken saute. To taste, incorporate pepper and salt.

Nutrition Facts (1 portion):

Energy: 464.1Kcal
Carbs: 66g
Proteins:8.4g

8. Chicken Protein Pots

Portion Size: 2
Duration: 35 min

Ingredients:

1/4 cup. carrots
2 tsp. butter
1/4 cups frozen sweet peas
1 egg (beaten)
1/2 tsp garlic powder
1/4-pound boneless chicken breast (cooked, chopped into 1/2-inch dice)
1/2 small onion, chopped
2 tbsp. soy sauce
Dash. of sea salt and black pepper

Instructions:

Butter should be melted over medium heat in a large nonstick pan.
Cook the carrots, peas, and onions until soft.
Eggs should be poured over the veggies once they have been pushed to one side. The eggs should be scrambled until they are set.
Combine the vegetables and the eggs.
Stir in the garlic powder and soy sauce.
Put the cooked chicken and rice in there. Mix thoroughly.
Green onions, some salt, and pepper are optional toppings. Enjoy!

Nutrition Facts (1 portion):

Energy: 162Kcal
Carbs: 6.7g
Proteins: 16g
Fats: 8.4g

9. Air fried chicken general Tso's burger

Portion Size: 2
Duration: 35 min

Ingredients:

1 small egg
½ lb. boneless, without skin chicken thighs,
1/4 cup cornstarch
1/8 tsp of kosher salt & white pepper, ground
3 Tbsps. Low-salt chicken broth
1 tbsp Low-sodium soy sauce.
1 spoonful of ketchup
1 tsp of sugar
1 Tbsp of rice vinegar that is unseasoned
1/2 Tbsp Canola oil
1 tsp of garlic and ginger, cut coarsely.
2 tbsp. sliced green onion
1 tsp. toasted sesame oil

Instructions:

In a large mixing basin, whisk the egg. Coat the chicken thoroughly. Add 1/3 cup corn flour, salt, and pepper to another bowl. With a fork, put the chicken to the corn flour mixture and coat it with it. When transferring the chicken to the air-fryer oven racks, leave a little space between each piece. Preheat the air fryer to 400°F for three minutes. Cook for 12 to 16 minutes, shaking the pan halfway through, with the chicken in the batter. Allow 3–5 minutes for drying. If one side of the chicken is still wet, cook it for another one to two minutes. Broth, soy sauce, ketchup, sugar, and rice vinegar are stirred together, along with the remaining 2 tablespoons corn flour. Heat the canola oil in a large skillet over medium heat.
Cook for about 30 seconds, or until the ginger and garlic are aromatic.
After beating the corn flour mixture, stir it in the skillet. Increase the heat to medium-high. Once the sauce has begun to bubble, add the chicken. Stir everything together and cook for 1 1/2 minutes. After the heat is turned off, add 1/2 teaspoon green onion and sesame oil. Transfer to a serving tray and top with the remaining 1/2 teaspoon green onion.

Nutrition Facts (1 portion):
Energy: 302Kcal
Carbs: 18g
Proteins: 26g
Fats: 13g

10. Chicken club wraps

Portion Size: 2
Duration: 35 min

Ingredients:

1/2 lbs. of cut, skinless, boneless chicken breast
1/4 tsp divided freshly ground pepper
3Tbsps of plain, nonfat Greek yogurt
3 Tbsps., Cider vinegar
3 tsps. minced onion
1 tbsp. extra-virgin olive oil
1/2 diced medium tomato
1/2 chop avocado
4 leaves of green leaf lettuce
2 10-inch whole wheat tortilla wraps

Instructions:
Preheat the grill to medium-high.
On both sides, season the chicken with 1/8 teaspoon pepper. Grease the grill rack with cooking spray. Grill the chicken for 15 to 18 minutes, rotating once or twice. Allow the food to cool for 5 minutes on a clean cutting board after transferring. Meanwhile, combine the remaining 1/8 teaspoon pepper with the yogurt, vinegar, onion, oil, salt, and a large mixing bowl. After chopping the chicken, tomato, and avocado into bite-sized pieces, toss them in the bowl.
Add 2 lettuce leaves before spreading the chicken salad on the tortillas. (1 cup per wrap). Roll up like a tortilla. Serve cut in half if desired.

Nutrition Facts (1 portion):
Energy: 526Kcal
Carbs: 39g
Proteins: 34g
Fats: 26g

11. Chicken Stew in a Skillet
Portion Size: 2
Duration: 35 min

Ingredients:
1/6 cup flour
3/4 lbs. boneless skinless chicken breasts
salt and pepper to taste
1 1/2 Tbsps. of butter
1/2 clove minced garlic
1 1/2 medium potatoes & carrots, peeled, sliced
1/2 medium onion, sliced
a 14 oz. can of chicken broth,
1 1/2 Tbsps. of flour

Instructions:

Cut the chicken into bite-sized pieces—roughly 1 piece.
Chicken is salted, peppered, and dusted in flour.
Melt the butter and cook the chicken in a big skillet.
Once added, cook the onion and garlic until soft.
Put in carrots and potatoes and stir.
Add the broth after stirring in the flour, and then bring to a boil.
When vegetables are soft, lower the heat, cover the pan, and simmer for 30 minutes.

Nutrition Facts (1 portion):
Energy: 516Kcal
Carbs: 50g
Proteins: 40g
Fats:17g

12. Chicken Shashlik
Portion Size: 2
Duration: 120 min

Ingredients:

250g chicken breast fillets, sliced
salt
1/2 tsp roughly chopped garlic
1/2 tsp coarsely chopped gingerroot
1/2 tsp ground cumin
1 tsp chili powder
1 tbsp. olive oil
1 small onion slices
1 medium capsicum, slice into 2-inch piece
1/4 tsp chat masala
2 tbsp. Low-fat plain yogurt

Instructions:

Cut the chicken into cubes. Salt should be added to the chicken before folding and setting it aside. Put the garlic, ginger, cumin, turmeric, and chili powder in a blender.
Make a smooth paste by blending in the yogurt. Add this to the chicken and let it sit for two hours, ideally overnight. Put the chicken in a pan and cook it in oil over high heat. Once the chicken is tender, lower the heat. Heat some oil in another frying pan. Cook the onions to a deep golden brown over medium heat. For further 4 minutes, sauté the capsicum on low to medium heat after adding it. Include this mixture with the cooked chicken.

Nutrition Facts (1 portion):
Energy: 421Kcal
Carbs: 27g
Proteins: 21g
Fats: 27.5g

13. Fried Chicken

Portion Size: 2
Duration: 30 min

Ingredients:

1 cup cut broiler-fryer chicken
1/4 cup of dry whole wheat bread crumbs
1 tbsp. salt
½ tbsp. paprika
¼ tbsp. Pepper
¼ cup of butter or olive oil.

Instructions:

Mix the paprika, salt, crumbs of bread, and pepper.
Brush butter or olive oil on the chicken pieces using a kitchen brush.
Roll the chicken in the breadcrumb mix.
Place the chicken pieces in a greased baking pan.
Bake the chicken at 425°F until it turns tender.
Serve it with mint sauce or homemade tomato salsa to enhance its taste and enrich its nutritional value.

Nutrition Facts (1 portion):

Energy: 453Kcal
Carbs: 35g
Proteins: 70g
Fats: 16g

14. Crispy Skinned Baked Chicken Drumstick

Portion Size: 2
Duration: 55 min

Ingredients:

8 (120g each) skin-on chicken drumsticks
2 tbsp. olive oil
1 tsp diamond crystal kosher salt
½ tsp. black pepper
1 tsp. garlic powder
1 tsp, onion powder
1 tsp smoked paprika
¼ tsp cayenne pepper

Instructions:

Turn the oven's temperature up to 400 degrees. Drumsticks should be arranged on parchment paper that has been highly heat resistant and covered in a single layer.
To make the seasoning paste, stir together the olive oil, spices, pepper, and herbs in a medium basin with a fork or spatula.
Apply the spice paste to the pieces of chicken. Drumsticks should be baked with the lid off for about 40 minutes or until the interior temperature reaches 165 degrees F. Apply pan juice to the drumsticks. Serve immediately.

Nutrition Facts (1 portion):

Energy: 288Kcal
Carbs: 10g
Proteins: 28g
Fats: 18 g

15. Pon Pon Chicken

Portion Size: 2
Duration: 25 min

Ingredients:

2 boneless chicken breasts
4 sliced cucumbers
1 Tbsp of salt
2 Tbsps. sesame seed paste or 1 Tbsp oil
5 tbsp. soy sauce
3 tsps. of sugar
2 tbsp. vinegar
3 tbsp. of Worcestershire sauce
1/2 tsp. of garlic & ginger juice
Black pepper, 2 dashes
a tsp of corn flour

Instructions:

Chicken can be steam- or poached-cooked for 10 to 12 minutes at medium heat.
Remove and permit cooling. then cut or shred into strips that are the same size.
Set apart.
Cucumbers should be peeled, split lengthwise in half, and then sliced into thin strips.
Combine 1/2 tsp salt and gently squeeze for one minute in a large basin.
Place evenly on a dish after thoroughly draining.
The dressing mix should be put in a pan with water, and it should be stirred as it slowly boils.
If necessary, include stock or water.

Nutrition Facts (1 portion):
Energy: 444Kcal
Carbs: 21g
Proteins: 59g
Fats: 15g

16. Thai Chicken Curry

Portion Size: 2
Duration: 25 min

Ingredient:

1 tbsps. of vegetable oil
1/2 tsp. curry paste
5/8 pound of cut-up, flesh from a skinless, boneless chicken breast
½ onion, crushed up coarsely
1/2 of red bell pepper, sliced
1/2 cup light coconut milk and
1/2 tbsp. lemon zest, shredded
Fish sauce, 1/2 tbsp.
1/2 tbsp. of fresh lime juice.
1/6 cup of fresh cilantro, cut finely

Instructions:

Heat the oil in a large skillet over high heat for about thirty seconds before pouring the curry paste. Cook for a further 3 minutes after adding the chicken. Stirring the bell pepper, onion, coconut cream, and lemon juice, fish sauce into the chicken, heat until the chicken is thoroughly cooked.
Stir after adding cilantro to the dish.
Serve warm.

Nutrition Facts (1 portion):

Energy: 343 Kcal
Carbs: 8.3 g
Proteins: 30 g
Fats: 22 g

17. Baked Salsa Chicken

Portion Size: 2

Duration: 85 min

Ingredients:

3/4 cup tomatoes
1 big onion or 1/4 cup of onions
3/4 Tbsps. of garlic
1/2 cups avocado
1/8 cup of lime juice
juice from half a lime, salt, and pepper.
1/4 lb. of chicken breast
A half-cup of long-grain rice
1 cup of chicken broth

Instructions:

Set the oven to 400 °F.
Chop avocado, cilantro, chives, tomatoes, onion, and garlic.
Combine chopped vegetables and lime juice in a prep container. To taste, add salt and pepper; put away.
Put butter or olive oil in a 13 x 9-inch glass baking dish to grease it.
Pour uncooked rice evenly onto the blazing dish's bottom.
Put the chicken breast on top of the rice.
Add chicken stock to the rice and chicken.
Top the chicken with the salsa mixture.
Wrap in aluminum foil.
Bake for one hour in the oven.

Nutrition Facts (1 portion):

Energy: 173 Kcal
Carbs: 24g
Proteins: 14g
Fats: 19g

18. Roast chicken breast with Garbanzo beans

Portion Size: 2

Duration: 35 min

Ingredients:

1/8 cup extra virgin olive oil
2 squeezed garlic cloves
1/2 Tbsps. of smoked paprika
1/2 tsps. ground cumin
1/4 tsp of dried, crushed red pepper
14 cups plain yogurt
1 pair of bone-in chicken breast halves
8 oz. can of drained garbanzo beans (chickpeas)
6.5 oz. jar cherry tomatoes
1/2 cup split fresh cilantro, chopped

Instructions:

Preheat the oven to 450°F. Combine the first 5 ingredients in a medium mixing basin. 1 tsp of the spicy oil mixture in a small bowl; stir in the yogurt and set aside for the sauce. Place the chicken on a rimmed baking sheet. 2 tablespoons of the spicy oil mixture should be sprinkled over the chicken. Add beans, tomatoes, and 1/2 cup cilantro to the remaining seasoned oil mixture. To mix, toss everything together. Spread the bean mixture around the chicken. Season everything thoroughly with salt and pepper.
Roast for about 20 minutes after the chicken is thoroughly cooked, adding half a cup of cilantro. Place the chicken on individual plates. Top with the bean mixture. Serve with the yogurt sauce on the side.

Nutrition Facts (1 portion):

Energy: 364Kcal
Carbs: 33g
Proteins: 12g
Fats: 21g

19. Grilled Chicken with White BBQ Sauce

Portion Size: 2
Duration: 35 min

Ingredients:

1 lb. assorted chicken parts
Parsley leaves, for garnish
1 recipe White BBQ Sauce
White BQQ Sauce
1/2 tbsp. horseradish drained
1/4 tbsp. lemon juice
1/8 c. cider vinegar
1/4 tsp. sugar
1/8 c. mayonnaise
1/8 tsp. cayenne (ground red) pepper

Instructions:

Set the grill to medium-low heat. Add 1 1/2 tsps. of salt and 1/2 tsp of black pepper to the chicken all over. Cook the chicken on the grill for 20 minutes while covering it.
Make White BBQ Sauce while the chicken is grilling. All Ingredients should be thoroughly combined after adding 3/4 tsp salt and 1/2 tsp black pepper.
In a bowl, put 34 cups of White BBQ Sauce. Chicken should be exposed; liberally sauce. Flip over the chicken pieces. Chicken should be cooked thoroughly (160°F) after 5 minutes of cooking, rotating and coating the chicken twice more.
Parsley is used as a garnish. Serve with any leftover sauce.

Nutrition Facts (1 portion):

Energy: 374 Kcal
Carbs: 15g
Proteins: 30g
Fats: 28g

20. Chicken quinoa bowl with olives and cucumber

Portion Size: 2
Duration: 35 min

Ingredients:

1/8 tsp Salt.
1 cup Quinoa
1/8 tsp Ground pepper
1/8 cup Slivered almond
1/6 tsp. Paprika
3oz. Red pepper roasted
1/8cup Pitted Kalamata olives
2 tbsp. Extra virgin olive oil
1/8 cup red onion
½ Cucumber diced
1/8 cup Fresh mozzarella Cheese
1 Tbsp. Fresh parsley

Instructions:

Place a baking tray in the upper third of the oven with the grill set to high. Make a foil rim to go around a baking sheet. Before placing the chicken on the preheated roasting pan, it should be seasoned and peppered. In the meantime, put the almonds, garlic, 2 tablespoons oil, almonds, paprika, crushed red pepper, and cumin (if using) in a small food processor. Blend when the mixture is largely smooth. In a medium mixing bowl, combine the quinoa, olives, and red onion with the remaining two tablespoons of oil. When you're ready to serve, divide the quinoa mixture into four bowls. Distribute the red pepper sauce, chicken, and cucumber in equal parts on top. Feta and parsley should be used as garnishes.

Nutrition Facts (1 portion):

Energy: 481Kcal
Carbs: 31g
Proteins: 34g
Fats: 27g

21. Chicken Quinoa Casserole

Portion Size: 2
Duration: 35 min

Ingredients:

½ clove Garlic
1 cup Chicken cooked & cubed
1/3 cup Quinoa
3 oz. Mushroom
1/3 tbsp. Olive oil
7 oz. Black beans
and Spices according to taste

Instructions:

Follow the package directions for quinoa preparation. Cooked chicken should be cut into bite-sized pieces. Open a small can of mushrooms, drain them, and use fresh mushrooms if available. After opening the black bean can, drain it (briefly rinse with cold water). If necessary or preferred, garlic, paprika, pepper, and other spices can be added.
If it appears to be a touch dry, a small layer of olive oil will help. Combine everything in a casserole dish and serve. If any of the ingredients are cold, warm everything before serving in a low oven or on the stovetop. I occasionally zap everything in the microwave to fully heat it all. If it appears to be a touch dry, a small layer of olive oil will help. Combine everything in a casserole dish and serve. If any of the ingredients are cold, reheat everything before serving, either in a low oven or in a stovetop saucepan. I occasionally zap stuff in the microwave to properly warm it up.

Nutrition Facts (1 portion):
Energy: 256Kcal
Carbs: 16g
Proteins: 21g
Fats: 12g

22. Baked Chicken Tenders

Portion Size: 2
Duration: 35 min

Ingredients:

2 skinless, boneless chicken breast halves
1 egg white, lightly beaten
1/2 tbsp. water
1/2 tsp finely shredded lemon peel
¼ cup. seasoned fine dry breadcrumb
1/8 cup finely shredded Parmesans cheese

Instructions:

Preheat the oven to 400 degrees Fahrenheit. Line a large baking sheet with rim with butter paper. Set away. Cooking spray should be used sparingly. Each chicken breast half should be cut into three lengthwise segments.
In a small bowl, combine the egg whites, water, and lemon peel. In a separate small bowl, combine the cheese and bread crumbs. Dip the chicken strips in the egg white mixture before covering them with bread crumbs. Arrange the strips on the prepared baking sheet. More frying oil should be poured on the chicken strips.
Bake for about 15 minutes, or until the chicken is no longer pink in the center (165 degrees F). If desired, serve with barbecue sauce.

Nutrition Facts (1 portion):
Energy: 207 Kcal
Carbs: 11g
Proteins: 32g
Fats: 3g

23. Chicken Quesadilla

Portion Size: 2
Duration: 35 min

Ingredients:

2 chicken breasts
2/5 onion diced
1/3 can green chili
1/3 package taco seasoning mix
Salsa, cheese to taste
2 tortillas

Instructions:

Chicken is chopped up and browned with diced onions.
Add salsa, taco seasoning mix, and green chilies.
Tortillas are cut in half, then filled.
Slice tortillas in half.
Spray a frying pan with nonstick spray, then lightly fry the tortilla on both sides.

Nutrition Facts (1 portion):

Energy: 53Kcal
Carbs: 5.4g
Proteins: 2.3g
Fats: 2.4g

24. Chicken Jalfrezi

Portion Size: 2
Duration: 65 min

Ingredients:

2/3 tbsp. vegetable oil
1/3 onion. sliced
2/3 cloves of garlic
1/2 lb. boneless skinless chicken thighs, cut in half
1 tsp turmeric
1/3 tsp chili. powder
1/2 tsp salt
1/3 can peel and sliced tomato
2/3 tbsp. butter
1 tsp ground cumin
1 tsp powdered coriander
2/3 tbsp. grated fresh ginger

Instructions:

In a large deep skillet, heat the oil over medium-high heat. Cook for about two minutes with the onions and garlic. After adding the chicken, season it with salt, turmeric, and chili powder. Cook the chicken gently, flipping it over as needed and scraping the bottom of the pan. Cover the pan, add the tomatoes, and cook for 20 minutes over medium heat. The surplus liquid will have evaporated after 10 minutes of boiling without the cover.
Continue to cook for 5 to 7 minutes after adding the ghee, ginger, and cumin. Serve the chicken pieces with the sauce on top.

Nutrition Facts (1 portion):

Energy: 602Kcal
Carbs: 5.18g
Proteins: 12 g
Fats: 56g

25. Chicken Patties with mashed potato

Portion Size: 2
Duration: 35 min

Ingredients:

170g chicken breast chopped by hand
1 ½ tbsp. parsley
1 spring onions
½ tsp butter
20g bread crumbs
Salt and pepper

For The Swede and Potato Mash
1 medium boiled potato
¼ cup boiled Swede
30g cheddar cheese
1 garlic clove, chopped finely, Salt

Instructions:

In a small frying pan, soften the spring onions with the butter; do not let them brown. Cool.
Add the chicken, parsley, breadcrumbs, salt, paper, and spring onions.
Shape that mixture into patties form by hand.
Fry then in oil until turns light brown.

For The Swede and Potato Mash
Boil potato and swede until got softens and then mash them.
Add the garlic grated, add grated cheese
Use a potato masher to mash, then taste for seasoning.

Nutrition Facts (1 portion):

Energy: 364 Kcal
Carbs: 33g
Proteins: 34g
Fats: 10.6g

Beef

1. Black Bean and Beef Tostadas

Portion Size: 2
Duration: 30 min

Ingredients:

1/4-pound lean ground beef
1/2 can black beans, rinsed
1/2 can diced tomatoes and green chiles
1/2 can of refried beans, warmed
4 tostada shells

Instructions:

Cook the beef for 4-6 min. Crumble the cooked steak. Put in the tomatoes and boil. Reduce heat and cook with the lid on until liquid nearly completely evaporates (6-8 min). Add black beans and heat well.
Tostada shells should be covered with refried beans for serving. Top with beef mixture and any preferred garnishes.

Nutrition Facts (1 portion):

Energy: 392 Kcal
Carbs: 46 g
Proteins:23 g
Fats: 14 g

2. Tomato Hamburger Soup

Portion Size: 2
Duration: 4 hrs.

Ingredients:

7.6 oz V8 juice
5 oz each frozen mixed vegetable
0.16-pound ground beef, cooked and drained
1.6 oz condensed cream of mushroom soup
1/2 tsps. dried minced onion
Pepper and salt

Instructions:

Combine all ingredients except seasoning in a 5-qt slow cooker for 4-5 hours on high, with the lid on, or until well heated. Incorporate pepper and salt as desired.

Nutrition Facts (1 portion):

Energy: 125 Kcal
Carbs: 9 g
Proteins:12 g
Fats: 5 g

3. Burger Americana

Portion Size: 2
Duration: 25 min

Ingredients:

¼ cup seasoned bread crumbs
1/2 large egg, lightly beaten
¼ tsp salt
¼ tsp pepper
½ pound ground beef
½ Tbsp olive oil
2 sesame seed hamburger buns
Toppings

Instructions:

Mix the egg, salt, bread crumbs, and pepper in a big container. Add steak and stir just enough to combine. Four patties (half-inch thick) should be formed. With your thumb, make a small depression in the middle of each patty. Oil should be brushed on patties on both sides.
Burgers should be broiled or grilled covered on medium till an instant-read thermometer registers 160° (4-5 min). Serve with toppings on buns.

Nutrition Facts (1 portion):

Energy: 429 Kcal
Carbs: 32 g
Proteins:28 g
Fats: 20 g

4. Asian Beef and Noodles

Portion Size: 2
Duration: 20 min

Ingredients:

½ pound lean ground beef
1 package Soy sauce ramen noodles, crumbled
1 cups water
1 cup frozen broccoli stir-fry vegetable blend
1/8 tsp ginger, minced
1 Tbsp green onion, sliced

Instructions:

Cook the meat on medium heat till it's not pink. Shred the beef. One package of ramen noodle flavoring should be added and stirred until it is dissolved. Remove and reserve the beef. Combine the water, vegetables, ginger, noodles, and the remaining flavoring packet's contents in the same skillet and boil. Lower the heat and cook with the lid on and occasionally stirring until noodles are done. Heat up the beef again. Mix onion in it.

Nutrition Facts (1 portion):

Energy: 383 Kcal
Carbs: 29 g
Proteins:27 g
Fats: 16 g

5. Smothered Burritos

Portion Size: 2
Duration: 30 min

Ingredients:

½ can (5 oz) green enchilada sauce
½ cup salsa verde
½ pound ground beef
4 2flour tortillas (10 inches)
1 cup shredded cheddar cheese, divided

Instructions:

Turn the oven on to 375 degrees. Mix the salsa verde and enchilada sauce in a small basin.
In a large skillet, cook the meat over medium heat (8-10min), and crumble it. Remove water. Stir in a half cup of the sauce mixture.
Each tortilla should have 2/3 cup of the beef mix, followed by 3 tbsp cheese. Fold the tortilla. Place in an oiled baking tray. Add the remaining sauce mixture and 3/4 cup of the cheese. Bake for 10-15 minutes.

Nutrition Facts (1 portion):

Energy: 624 Kcal
Carbs: 44 g
Proteins: 36 g
Fats: 33 g

6. Beef and Broccoli

Portion Size: 2
Duration: 15 min

Ingredients:
8 oz. flank steak, thinly sliced
2 cups broccoli florets
1 tbsp. vegetable oil
1 tbsp. soy sauce
1 tsp. cornstarch
1 tbsp. oyster sauce
Salt and pepper, to taste
1/4 tsp. garlic powder

Instructions:
Mix garlic powder, pepper, sauces, cornstarch, and salt. Add sliced beef in warmed oil and brown it. Add broccoli in the pan and cook until the broccoli is tender but still crisp. Put in soy sauce mixture. Stir to thicken it so it coats the beef and broccoli evenly. Serve with cooked rice.

Nutrition Facts (1 portion):
Energy: 305 Kcal
Carbs: 14 g
Proteins: 33 g
Fats: 13 g

7. Slow Cooker Beef Stew

Portion Size: 2
Duration: 4 hrs.

Ingredients:

1 lb. beef stew meat
2 cups chopped mixed vegetables (such as carrots, Potatoes, and onions)
1 can (14 oz.) diced tomatoes, undrained
1 cup beef broth
1 tbsp. Worcestershire sauce
Salt and pepper, to taste

Instructions:

Place beef stew meat, mixed vegetables, salt, beef broth, Worcestershire sauce, tomatoes, and salt in a slow cooker.
Mix everything together.
Cook (4-5 hrs.) until the beef and vegetables are cooked through.
Serve hot.

Nutrition Facts (1 portion):

Energy: 337 Kcal
Carbs: 31 g
Proteins: 33 g
Fats: 9 g

8. Beef and Vegetable Soup Recipe

Portion Size: 2
Duration: 35 min

Ingredients:

8 oz. beef stew meat
2 cloves garlic, minced
2 cups mixed vegetables (such as carrots, celery, and potatoes)
4 cups beef broth
1 onion, chopped
Pepper and Salt

Instructions:

Brown the beef stew meat at medium heat along with garlic and onion until cooked thoroughly (5 mins)
Put mixed vegetables and beef broth in the pot.
Boil everything, and simmer until the vegetables are cooked through (20 mins).
Add pepper and salt. Enjoy warm.

Nutrition Facts (1 portion):

Energy: 236 Kcal
Carbs: 8 g
Proteins: 22 g
Fats: 8 g

9. Beef and Guinness Stew

Portion Size: 2
Duration: 2-3 hrs.

Ingredients:

1 lb. beef stew meat
2 cloves garlic, minced
2 celery stalks, chopped
1 onion, chopped
1/2 cup Guinness beer
2 carrots, chopped
1 cup beef broth
1 bay leaf
1 tbsp. tomato paste
1 tsp. dried thyme
Pepper and salt

Instructions:

Brown the beef stew meat along with onion and garlic until cooked through (5-7 mins). Cook carrots and celery in the pot (5-7 mins) until slightly softened. Pour in the Guinness beer with beef broth and stir to combine.
Mix thyme, bay leaf, salt, pepper and tomato paste in it. Simmer it, and lower the to simmer until the meat is soft (1-2 hrs.) and the flavors have melded together. Serve hot.

Nutrition Facts (1 portion):

Energy: 397 Kcal
Carbs: 17 g
Proteins: 42 g
Fats: 14 g

10. Beef and Sweet Potato Curry

Portion Size: 2
Duration: 30 min

Ingredients:

1 lb. beef sirloin, thinly sliced
1 onion, chopped
1 sweet potato, peeled and chopped
1 can (14 oz.) coconut milk
2 cloves garlic, minced
1 tbsp. curry powder
Pepper and salt

Instructions:

Cook the beef sirloin with onion as well as garlic until cooked through (3-4 mins).
Remove the beef and put in sweet potato to cook (7 mins).
Add the salt, curry powder, pepper, and coconut milk and combine.
Add the beef back and stir everything together. Simmer, lower the heat, and Simmer again until the sweet potato is fully cooked (20 mins) and the flavors have melded together.
Serve hot

Nutrition Facts (1 portion):

Energy: 541 Kcal
Carbs: 22 g
Proteins: 35 g
Fats: 35 g

11. Beef and Spinach Lasagna

Portion Size: 2
Duration: 30 min

Ingredients:

4 lasagna noodles
1/2 lb. ground beef
1/2 cup marinara sauce
1/2 cup ricotta Cheese
1/2 cup Shredded mozzarella Cheese
1 cup spinach, chopped
Pepper and Salt

Instructions:

Preheat the oven (370°F). Boil noodles as per box instructions. Cook ground beef over medium heat. Drain any excess fat.
Put in marinara sauce to the skillet and stir to combine. In another bowl, mix together ricotta cheese, shredded mozzarella cheese, chopped spinach, salt, and pepper. Assemble the lasagna by spreading a layer of the meat sauce on the bottom of a small baking dish. Add a layer of cooked lasagna noodles, then a layer of the ricotta cheese mixture. Repeat layers.
Bake until cheese is bubbly (20 min).

Nutrition Facts (1 portion):

Energy: 468 Kcal
Carbs: 37 g
Proteins: 29 g
Fats: 21 g

12. Beef and Cabbage Soup

Portion Size: 2
Duration: 25 min

Ingredients:

1/2 lb. ground beef
2 cups beef broth
1 cup water
1 chopped cup cabbage,
1/2 chopped cup carrot,
1/2 chopped cup celery,
1/2 chopped cup onion,
1 clove garlic, minced
1 bay leaf
Pepper and salt

Instructions:

Cook minced beef in a saucepan and remove any extra fat.
Add beef broth, water, chopped cabbage, carrot, celery, onion, salt, bay leaf, pepper, and garlic to a saucepan. Boil, then simmer at low heat (20 mins). Remove bay leaf before enjoying.

Nutrition Facts (1 portion):

Energy: 191 Kcal
Carbs: 8 g
Proteins: 15 g
Fats: 11 g

13. Beef and Cheese Quesadillas

Portion Size: 2
Duration: 15 min

Ingredients:

2 flour tortillas
1/2 lb. ground beef
1/2 cup shredded cheddar cheese
1/2 cup salsa
Pepper and Salt

Instructions:

Cook minced beef in a pan. Remove any extra fat. Add pepper and salt in it.
Put a tortilla in skillet. Top with cooked ground beef, shredded cheddar cheese, and salsa.
Place another tortilla on top and cook to, melt the cheese.
Toss the quesadilla and cook the other side.
Cut in quarters and enjoy.

Nutrition Facts (1 portion):

Energy: 459 Kcal
Carbs: 28 g
Proteins: 30 g
Fats: 24 g

14. Ravioli Lasagna

Portion Size: 2
Duration: 65 min

Ingredients:

1/4 lb. ground beef
¼ jar (28 oz) spaghetti sauce
6 oz frozen sausage or cheese ravioli
¼ cups shredded part-skim mozzarella cheese
Minced fresh basil, optional

Instructions:

Cook and crumble the beef in a big pan for 5-7 minutes; drain. Place 1/3 of the spaghetti sauce, 1/2 of the beef and ravioli, and 1/2 cup of cheese in a buttered baking dish. Repeat layers. Add cheese and the remaining sauce over it.
For 40–45 mins, bake with cover at 400° until thoroughly heated. Serve with basil on top, if preferred.

Nutrition Facts (1 portion):

Energy: 438 Kcal
Carbs: 42 g
Proteins: 26 g
Fats: 18 g

15. Mexican Stuffed Peppers

Portion Size: 2
Duration: 30 min

Ingredients:

1/4-pound lean ground beef
1/4 envelope of Mexican-style rice and pasta mix
1/4 cups water
2 medium sweet peppers
1/4 can diced tomatoes and green chiles, undrained
1/2 cup shredded Mexican cheese blend, divided
Minced fresh cilantro

Instructions:

Set oven to 375 degrees. Cook and shred the beef for 5-7 minutes; drain. Tomatoes, rice mixture, and water are stirred in. Boil. Lower heat; simmer it covered for 6 to 8 mins.
Remove the peppers' tops and throw them away. Peppers should be put in a buttered baking dish. Each pepper should have 1/3 cup of the meat mixture, then add 2 tsps. of cheese. the leftover rice mixture on top. 25 minutes of covered baking. Add the remaining cheese. Bake uncovered for 5 to 10 mins. Add cilantro on top if you like.

Nutrition Facts (1 portion):
Energy: 301 Kcal
Carbs: 23 g
Proteins: 20 g
Fats: 14 g

16. Pizza Roll-Ups

Portion Size: 2
Duration: 35 min

Ingredients:

¼ pound ground beef
½ can tomato sauce
¼ tsp dried oregano
1 tube refrigerated crescent rolls
¼ cup shredded part-skim mozzarella cheese

Instructions:

Cook the beef and drain. Get rid of the heat. Put in mozzarella cheese, oregano, and tomato sauce. Make 4 rectangles out of the crescent dough by squeezing the seams together. Along one long side of each rectangle, spread roughly 3 Tbsps. of the meat mixture. Starting with a long side, roll it like a jellyroll. Divide each roll into three pieces.
Place on buttered baking pans, seam side down at a distance of 2 inches. Bake for 15 mins at 375 degrees.

Nutrition Facts (1 portion):

Energy: 94 Kcal
Carbs: 9 g
Proteins: 4 g
Fats: 5 g

17. Beefy Tortellini Skillet

Portion Size: 2
Duration: 20 min

Ingredients:

½ pound ground beef
¼ tsp Montreal steak seasoning
½ cup water
½ tsp beef bouillon granules
½ package (8 oz) frozen cheese tortellini
½ cup shredded Italian cheese blend

Instructions:

Using a pan, sauté the beef (5 to 6 mins). Shred the meat and drain. Put in steak spice and mix. Bring bouillon and water to a boil. Tortellini is added after stirring, and the water is then boiled. Cook the tortellini at low heat for 3–4 mins with lid on.
Top with cheese and let it melt.

Nutrition Facts (1 portion):

Energy: 566 Kcal
Carbs: 37 g
Proteins: 39 g
Fats: 28 g

18. Super Spaghetti Sauce

Portion Size: 2
Duration: 30 min

Ingredients:

½ lb. ground beef
½ lb. smoked kielbasa, sliced
1 jar (12 oz each) spaghetti sauce with mushrooms
½ jar (8 oz) chunky salsa
Hot cooked pasta

Instructions:

Beef should be cooked in a Dutch oven, then it should be drained and placed aside. Sausage should be cooked in the same pan for 5 to 6 min at medium heat.
Put in the spaghetti sauce, salsa, and beef that was set aside; heat through. Served alongside pasta.

Nutrition Facts (1 portion):

Energy: 325 Kcal
Carbs: 18 g
Proteins: 17 g
Fats: 21 g

19. Beef Stir-Fry with Vegetable

Portion Size: 2
Duration: 10 min

Ingredients:

8 oz. flank steak, thinly sliced against the grain
2 garlic cloves, minced
1 cup sliced mixed vegetables (such as bell peppers, carrots, and onions)
1 tbsp. vegetable oil
Pepper and Salt
1 tbsp. soy sauce

Instructions:

Warm the oil over medium heat. Put in sliced beef and cook until browned for 3 mins.
Add the mixed vegetables with minced garlic to the pan. Continue to cook for another 2 mins.
Add salt, soy sauce, pepper and stir to combine.
Enjoy with cooked rice.

Nutrition Facts (1 portion):

Energy: 320 Kcal
Carbs: 12 g
Proteins: 35 g
Fats: 14 g

20. Chili Con Carne

Portion Size: 2
Duration: 25 min

Ingredients:

1 lb. ground beef
1 can (14 oz.) diced tomatoes, undrained
1 onion, chopped
1 can (15 oz.) kidney beans, drained and rinsed
2 cloves garlic, minced
1 tbsp. chili powder
Pepper and salt
1 tsp. cumin

Instructions:

Cook the ground beef with garlic and onion until cooked through, about 5-7 mins. Remove extra fat.
Add the diced tomatoes, kidney beans, chili powder, cumin, pepper, and salt to the pan.
Mix everything and simmer.
Lower the heat and simmer for 10 mins until the flavors have melded together.
Serve hot.

Nutrition Facts (1 portion):

Energy: 467 Kcal
Carbs: 35 g
Proteins: 36 g
Fats: 23 g

21. Beef and Mushroom Stroganoff Recipe

Portion Size: 2
Duration: 25 min

Ingredients:

8 oz. beef sirloin, sliced
2 cloves garlic, minced
8 oz. mushrooms, sliced
1/2 cup beef broth
1/2 onion, chopped
1/2 cup sour cream
1 tbsp. vegetable oil
Pepper and Salt
1 tbsp. flour
Cooked egg noodles, for serving

Instructions:

Brown the beef sirloin with onion as well as garlic (3-4 mins). Take the meat out and put in mushrooms in the same pan and cook for 5 mi. Mix together beef broth, sour cream, and flour. Add the beef back to the pan with the mushrooms and add the sour cream mix to everything. Stir everything together and simmer. Lower the heat and simmer for 10 mins. Add pepper and salt. Enjoy with egg noodles.

Nutrition Facts (1 portion):

Energy: 412 Kcal
Carbs: 16 g
Proteins: 31 g
Fats: 25 g

22. Beef and Rice Skillet Recipe

Portion Size: 2
Duration: 30 min

Ingredients:

1 lb. ground beef
1 bell pepper, chopped
1 cup beef broth
1 onion, chopped
1 can (14 oz.) diced tomatoes, undrained
2 cloves garlic, minced
1 cup uncooked white rice
1 tsp. chili powder
Pepper and Salt

Instructions:

Cook the ground beef in a pan with onion as well as garlic until cooked through, for 5-7 minutes.
Remove any extra fat from the skillet.
Add the bell pepper, diced tomatoes, rice, beef broth, chili powder, pepper, and salt to the skillet.
Stir everything together and boil.
Cover the skillet, and simmer at low heat for 18-20 mins.
Serve hot.

Nutrition Facts (1 portion):

Energy: 580 Kcal
Carbs: 57 g
Proteins: 38 g
Fats: 21 g

23. French Onion Beef Soup

Portion Size: 2
Duration: 20 min

Ingredients:

1 tbsp olive oil
2 cups beef broth
1/4 cup shredded Gruyere cheese
1 large onion, sliced
1/2 cup red wine
1/2 lb. beef stew meat
1 tsp thyme
Pepper and Salt
1 bay leaf
1 slice of bread

Instructions:

Warm the olive oil. Add sliced onions and sauté till caramelized. Put in beef stew meat to the saucepan and cook until browned.
Put in beef broth, thyme, salt, bay leaf, pepper, and red wine to the saucepan. Boil, then simmer at low heat (30-40 mins).
Preheat the broiler. Put bread on a baking sheet and toast.
Place soup in a bowl that is oven safe. Put toasted bread and shredded Gruyere over it. Melt the cheese by broiling

Nutrition Facts (1 portion):

Energy: 386 Kcal
Carbs: 17 g
Proteins: 26 g
Fats: 21 g

24. Roasted Mango with Vanilla Yogurt

Portion Size: 2
Duration: 30 min

Ingredients:

1 mango
2 Tbsp Organic Pure Cane Light Brown Sugar
1 Tbsp Pure Olive Oil
Pepper to taste
1 1/2 Tbsp thinly sliced Mint
2 Tbsp Vanilla Low Fat Yogurt

Instructions:

Set oven to broil. Slice the unpeeled mango's wide sides away from the pit. Cube the meat, then gently invert the cubes to separate them. Put the scored mango halves (skin-side-down) in a shallow casserole tray. Top with brown sugar and olive oil. Use pepper to season.
Roast for 3 to 5 minutes on the highest rack of the oven. Add yogurt on top, then add mint as a garnish.

Nutrition Facts (1 portion):

Energy: 250 Kcal
Carbs: 50 g
Proteins: 3 g
Fats: 7 g

25. Classic Meatloaf

Portion Size: 2
Duration: 55 min

Ingredients:

1/2 lb. ground beef
1/4 cup milk
1/4 cup breadcrumbs
1 egg
1 clove garlic, minced
1/4 cup onion, chopped
1 tbsp Worcestershire sauce
Pepper and Salt

Instructions:

Set th3 oven (370°F) to preheat.
Mix together ground beef, breadcrumbs, milk, egg, chopped onion, minced garlic, Worcestershire sauce, salt, and pepper.
Combined well.
Shape the meat mixture into a loaf and put in an oiled loaf pan.
Bake in the preheated oven for 50-60 mins.

Nutrition Facts (1 portion):

Energy: 317 Kcal
Carbs: 11 g
Proteins: 23 g
Fats: 19 g

Pizza and Pasta Dishes

1. Spaghetti with Meatballs

Portion Size: 2
Duration: 20 min

Ingredients:

8 oz spaghetti
1/4 cup breadcrumbs
1/4 cup chopped fresh parsley
1/2 lb. ground beef
1 egg
1/4 cup grated Parmesan cheese
1/4 tsp salt
2 tbsp olive oil
24 oz of your favorite marinara sauce
1 garlic minced clove
1/4 tsp black pepper

Instructions:

Cook spaghetti as per box Instructions. Mix ground beef, breadcrumbs, salt, parsley, cheese, pepper, and egg until combined. Make meatballs from this mix (half inch in thickness). Warm olive oil and put in meatballs to brown them on all sides (6 min). Cook garlic until fragrant. Pour marinara sauce over the meatballs and simmer. Cook covered until meatballs are cooked through (10 mins). Serve meatballs and sauce over spaghetti.

Nutrition Facts (1 portion):

Energy: 344 Kcal
Carbs: 34 g
Proteins: 17 g
Fats: 15 g

2. Penne alla Vodka

Portion Size: 2
Duration: 25 min

Ingredients:

8 oz penne pasta
1/2 onion, chopped
1/4 cup vodka
1 tbsp olive oil
1 cup tomato sauce
1 garlic clove, minced
1/2 cup heavy cream
Fresh parsley, chopped
Pepper and salt

Instructions:

Cook penne pasta as per box instructions. Warm olive oil to put in chopped garlic with the onion. Sauté it for 5 mins. Pour in the vodka and reduce it halfway through cooking. Add tomato sauce and simmer. Stir in heavy cream pepper and salt. Add cooked penne pasta and combine until well coated. Enjoy hot, topped with chopped parsley.

Nutrition Facts (1 portion):

Energy: 305 Kcal
Carbs: 35 g
Proteins: 5 g
Fats: 13 g

3. Baked Ziti

Portion Size: 2
Duration: 50 min

Ingredients:
8 oz ziti pasta
1 cup ricotta Cheese
1/2 onion, chopped
1 jar (24 oz) tomato sauce
1/2 lb. ground beef
1/4 cup grated Parmesan cheese
1 cup shredded mozzarella cheese
1/4 cup chopped fresh parsley
2 garlic cloves, minced
Salt and pepper, to taste
1 cup shredded mozzarella cheese

Instructions:

Cook the ziti as directed. Cook ground beef, chopped onion, and minced garlic in a skillet for 7 mins. Add tomato sauce to skillet and simmer. In a separate container, mix ricotta, Parmesan, chopped parsley, salt, and pepper. Combined well. Layer cooked ziti, meat sauce, and ricotta mix in a baking dish. Repeat the layers. Put mozzarella on it. Place in oven (375°F) for 25 mins.
Serve hot.

Nutrition Facts (1 portion):

Energy: 515 Kcal
Carbs: 37 g
Proteins: 31 g
Fats: 27 g

4. Margherita Pizza

Portion Size: 2
Duration: 15 min

Ingredients:

1 (12-inch) pre-made pizza crust
1/2 cup shredded mozzarella cheese
6-8 fresh basil leaves, chopped
1/2 cup pizza sauce
2-3 Roma tomatoes, sliced
Pepper and salt
Olive oil for drizzling

Instructions:

Set oven to 425°F to preheat.
Put sauce all over the pizza crust.
Add shredded mozzarella and tomatoes over it.
Sprinkle chopped basil leaves.
Add pepper and salt. Drizzle with olive oil.
Bake until cheese is bubbly (10 mins).
Slice and serve hot.

Nutrition Facts (1 portion):

Energy: 205 Kcal
Carbs: 25 g
Proteins: 7 g
Fats: 9 g

5. Hawaiian Pizza

Portion Size: 2
Duration: 15 min

Ingredients:

1 (12-inch) pre-made pizza crust
1/4 cup canned pineapple tidbits, drained
1/2 cup pizza sauce
4 slices Canadian bacon, chopped
1 cup shredded mozzarella cheese
Pepper and salt

Instructions:

Set oven at 425°F to preheat.
Put sauce all on the crust.
Add shredded mozzarella over the sauce.
Put chopped Canadian bacon with drained pineapple tidbits on top of the cheese.
Season using pepper and salt.
Bake until cheese is bubbly (12 mins).
Slice and enjoy hot.

Nutrition Facts (1 portion):

Energy: 225 Kcal
Carbs: 20 g
Proteins: 11 g
Fats: 10 g

Portion Size: 2
Duration: 15 min

Ingredients:

1 pre-made pizza crust
1 cup shredded mozzarella cheese
1/2 onion, thinly sliced
1/2 cup tomato sauce
1/2 bell pepper, thinly sliced
1 tbsp olive oil
Pepper and salt

Instructions:

Set oven to 425°F to preheat.
Put sauce all over the crust.
Sprinkle shredded mozzarella on it.
Top with thinly sliced bell pepper and onion.
Add olive oil, pepper, and salt.
Bake until the cheese is bubbly (10 mins).

Nutrition Facts (1 portion):

Energy: 405 Kcal
Carbs: 41 g
Proteins: 18 g
Fats: 18 g

6. Vegetarian Pizza

7. Lemon Butter Pasta with Asparagus

Portion Size: 2
Duration: 15 min

Ingredients:

4 oz spaghetti
8 asparagus spears, trimmed and cut
1 tbsp lemon juice
2 tbsp butter
1 garlic clove, minced
Pepper and salt

Instructions:

Boil spaghetti as per box instructions (typically 8-10 minutes).
Put asparagus into boiling water (2-3 min).
Use a separate pan to cook butter with added lemon juice and garlic (1-2 minutes).
Put the pasta and asparagus in the pan containing sauce. Combine well.
Add pepper and salt. Enjoy warm.

Nutrition Facts (1 portion):

Energy: 302 Kcal
Carbs: 39 g
Proteins: 8 g
Fats: 13 g

Portion Size: 2
Duration: 15 min

Ingredients:

4 oz spaghetti
1/4 cup Grated parmesan Cheese
2 slices of bacon, chopped
1 egg
Pepper and salt

Instructions:

Boil the spaghetti as per box instructions (typically 8-10 minutes).
In a pan, cook the chopped bacon till crispy.
Whisk the parmesan cheese with the egg in the container.
Put in cooked spaghetti to pan with cooked bacon and combine well.
Put egg and parmesan mix in the pan and toss everything together.
Add pepper and salt. Enjoy.

Nutrition Facts (1 portion):

Energy: 406 Kcal
Carbs: 36 g
Proteins: 17 g
Fats: 20 g

8. Carbonara Spaghetti

9. Fettuccine Alfredo

Portion Size: 2
Duration: 30 min

Ingredients:

1/4 cup unsalted butter
8 oz fettuccine
1/2 cup grated Parmesan cheese
1/2 cup heavy cream
Pepper and salt, to taste
Fresh parsley, chopped

Instructions:

Boil fettuccine as per box instructions. Melt butter and put in heavy cream, and whisk till combined. Add grated Parmesan cheese and whisk till the sauce is smooth. Add pepper and salt as per preference.
Put cooked fettuccine in it and toss well.
Enjoy hot, garnished with chopped parsley (optional).

Nutrition Facts (1 portion):

Energy: 390 Kcal
Carbs: 24 g
Proteins: 11.5 g
Fats: 18.5 g

10. Garlic Shrimp Linguine

Portion Size: 2
Duration: 20 min

Ingredients:

8 oz linguine
4 garlic cloves, minced
1/4 cup white wine
1/4 cup unsalted butter
1/4 cup chicken broth
1/2 lb. shrimp, peeled and deveined
1/4 cup heavy cream
Fresh parsley, chopped
Pepper and salt

Instructions:

Cook linguine as per package Instructions.
Melt butter with minced garlic and sauté (1 min).
Put in shrimp cooked thoroughly for 3-4 mins.
Add white wine and broth and boil. Add heavy cream, pepper, and salt.
Put in cooked linguine to the sauce and toss until well coated. Enjoy warm, garnished with chopped parsley.

Nutrition Facts (1 portion):

Energy: 345 Kcal
Carbs: 30 g
Proteins: 12 g
Fats: 18 g

11. Creamy Chicken and Broccoli Alfredo

Portion Size: 2
Duration: 25 min

Ingredients:

8 oz fettuccine
2 tbsp unsalted butter
1 cup broccoli florets
1/2 cup heavy cream
2 cloves of garlic, minced
1/4 cup grated Parmesan cheese
1 lb. cubed, skinless, and boneless chicken breast
Pepper and salt

Instructions:

Boil pasta as per box instructions.
In a pan, melt the butter. Put in chicken to cook thoroughly for 7 mins.
Add broccoli florets with minced garlic to the skillet and cook until it's crispy.
Stir in the cheese and cream. Add pepper and salt.
Put in cooked fettuccine in the skillet and toss.

Nutrition Facts (1 portion):

Energy: 305 Kcal
Carbs: 24 g
Proteins: 16 g
Fats: 16 g

12. Pepperoni Pizza

Portion Size: 2
Duration: 15 min

Ingredients:

1/2 cup pizza sauce
1 cup Shredded mozzarella Cheese
1 (12-inch) pre-made pizza crust
16 slices Pepperoni
Pepper and salt

Instructions:

Set oven to 425°F to preheated.
Put BBQ sauce uniformly on pizza crust.
Add shredded mozzarella cheese on the top and arrange pepperoni slices over it.
Sprinkle salt and pepper as per taste.
Bake until cheese is bubbly (12 min).
Slice and enjoy hot.

Nutrition Facts (1 portion):

Energy: 260 Kcal
Carbs: 19 g
Proteins: 12 g
Fats: 15 g

13. BBQ Chicken Pizza

Portion Size: 2
Duration: 15 min

Ingredients:

1 pre-made pizza crust
1 tbsp olive oil
1/4 cup BBQ sauce
1/2 cup cooked chicken, shredded
1/4 red onion, thinly sliced
1/2 cup shredded mozzarella cheese

Instructions:

Set oven to 425°F to preheat.
Put BBQ sauce uniformly on the pizza crust.
Top with mozzarella, chicken, and red onion.
Add the olive oil.
Put in oven until the crust turns golden (15 mins).

Nutrition Facts (1 portion):

Energy: 475 Kcal
Carbs: 49 g
Proteins: 25 g
Fats: 20 g

14. Four Cheese Pizza

Portion Size: 2
Duration: 15 min

Ingredients:

1/2 cup crumbled feta cheese
1 pre-made pizza crust
1/2 cup tomato sauce
1/2 cup shredded Parmesan cheese
1 cup shredded mozzarella cheese
1/4 cup fresh basil leaves

Instructions:

Put dough on a pizza stone.
Uniformly cover it with tomato sauce.
Add shredded mozzarella cheese, Parmesan cheese, and crumbled feta cheese on it.
Add chopped fresh basil leaves.
In a 425°F oven, bake it for 12 to 15 mins. Enjoy!

Nutrition Facts (1 portion):

Energy: 460 Kcal
Carbs: 32 g
Proteins: 23 g
Fats: 28 g

15. Tomato and Basil Spaghetti Recipe:

Portion Size: 2
Duration: 15 min

Ingredients:

4 oz spaghetti
1/2 can tomatoes, diced
1 tbsp olive oil
1/4 tsp red pepper flakes
1 garlic clove
Fresh basil
Pepper and Salt

Instructions:

Cook spaghetti according to package instructions (typically 8 mins).
Warm the olive oil and put in garlic with red pepper flakes. After 2 mins, put in the pepper, diced tomatoes, and salt to the pan and stir for 7 mins, until the tomatoes release their juices.
Drain the cooked spaghetti and mix it with the tomato sauce. Coat it well.
Top with freshly chopped basil and serve immediately.

Nutrition Facts (1 portion):

Energy: 238 Kcal
Carbs: 36 g
Proteins: 7 g
Fats: 7 g

Conclusion:

Cooking on a gas grill is an excellent way to bring the flavor of an outdoor dinner to your backyard or patio. We hope that this cookbook will give you with a comprehensive reference to cooking on gas, covering everything from the benefits and characteristics of using a gas grill to tips and tricks for prepping and utilizing your grill. One of the most significant benefits of cooking on a gas barbecue is its simplicity. Gas grills, as opposed to traditional charcoal grills, provide exact temperature control, allowing you to cook your meal to perfection every time. As a result, gas grills are ideal for both novice and experienced grillers, as they give a dependable and consistent cooking experience. Gas grills are quite adaptable in addition to temperature control. You can grill, roast, smoke, and even bake on a gas barbecue with the correct equipment and accessories. This means you can cook everything from burgers and hot dogs to pizzas and desserts on your barbecue.

There are a few crucial tips and practices to remember when prepping and operating your gas barbecue. First and foremost, you should purchase a high-quality infrared thermometer, which will allow you to properly assess the temperature of your grill and food. You should also be careful where you set your meal on the grill, as different regions will be hotter or cooler than others. Cleaning your grill is another vital issue when grilling on gas. Regular cleaning is required to keep your grill in good operating order and to prevent the accumulation of grease and other debris. After each usage, we recommend cleaning your grill with a wire brush to remove any excess debris from the grates.

Finally, in this cookbook, we've included a variety of delectable recipes to help you get the most out of your gas grill. There's something for everyone on these pages, from breakfast and brunch dishes to appetizers, side dishes, salads, and main entrees. We've also included vegetarian and seafood options for people who choose not to consume meat. We hope that this cookbook has encouraged you to learn more about gas grilling and that you've picked up some new tips and tricks along the way. This book has something for everyone, whether you're a seasoned griller or a complete novice. So light your grill, take your tongs, and prepare to enjoy some great cuisine cooked on your gas barbecue. Have fun grilling!